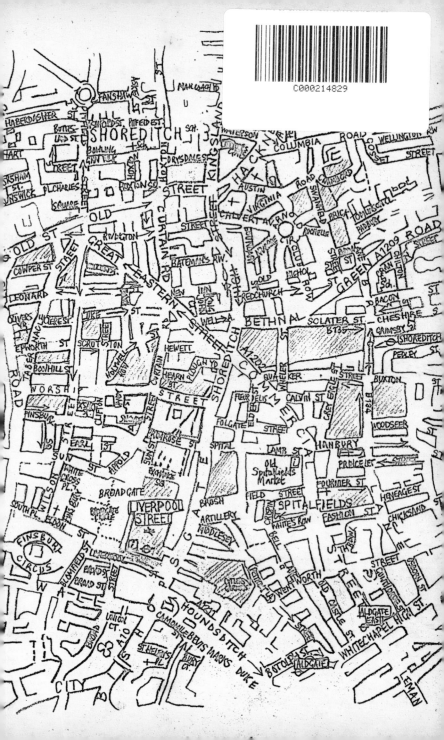

UNREQUITED
LOVE

UNREQUITED LOVE

ON STALKING AND BEING STALKED

a story of obsessive passion

BY GREGORY DART

✳ SHORT BOOKS

First published in 2003 by
Short Books
15 Highbury Terrace
London N5 1UP

10 9 8 7 6 5 4 3 2 1

A CIP catalogue record for this book
is available from the British Library.

ISBN 1-904095-28-3
Printed in Great Britain by
Bookmarque Ltd., Croydon, Surrey

I

She won't stop writing to me – e-mails, letters, texts, cards – but it's not merely because I hardly know her that I no longer reply. It is the increasingly demanding tone, and the fact that a romance is gaining momentum without my needing to be involved. Sometimes her complaints seem so plausible that I wonder if I am not the one to blame. At others, it is the pure flame of her hatred that mesmerises me, and I begin to feel afraid.

A stray bleat from my mobile phone and all at once I am vibrating in sympathy, lost in a wild abstraction of alarm. I WORRY ABOUT YOU. YOUR BEHAVIOUR IS NOT NORMAL. I walk away from the tube entrance and down a side street, entering an empty square overlooked by law offices. Bleached flagstones skitter and echo in every direction. A new text message presses its face to the glass. WE MUST SPEAK. EVERYTHING IS TOO OVERWROUGHT. It is impossible to ignore such bulletins, equally impossible to respond. I feel as if I am floating in a sea of white space, like a single point on a graph. And with each passing day the messages I receive from her, and from everyone else, become more vexed and impatient: I TRIED TO GET IN TOUCH WITH YOU YESTERDAY. WHY DON'T YOU EVER ANSWER YOUR PHONE?

I am a thirty-four-year-old lecturer in English literature, and Lucy, the woman in question, is a student working in the same field. The situation has, I admit, a suspicious ring to it; it has all the hallmarks of some catastrophic tutor-student affair. Things might be simpler if it was; certainly it would be far more evident who was to blame. But in spite of appearances, it is not that kind of story. I have never taught Lucy; she is not one of my undergraduates. She is a PhD student in her mid-twenties, based at a university hundreds of miles away.

Why, then, should I be so afraid of her? And why has she made me so wary of everyone else? Perhaps it is precisely because of the strange, rather abstract status she has in my life, being neither a former friend nor an ex-lover, that she has had such a crushing effect on my self-confidence, bringing all my other relationships into question. What makes matters worse is the fact that, even after a full year in London, many of my new friendships still feel extremely fluid and precarious, so that every move I make seems like a false one. How curious, then, that Lucy's capricious mixture of anger and appeal – the very thing that is making me feel so uncertain in relation to my new friends and colleagues – is fast becoming the sole element that I can depend on, the one ever-present in my life. So too, the fact that her complaints seem to come out of nowhere has accorded them a strange kind of authority. They descend upon me when I least expect them, like judgments from heaven. I HAVE DONE NOTHING TO DESERVE THIS. I CAN'T IMAGINE FEELING THE COLDNESS OR LACK OF COMPASSION YOU SEEM TO FEEL TOWARDS ME. On receiving such messages, I am filled with indignation, and in the very intensity of my reaction, I become convinced that she is being unjust. Not only unjust but unjustified: without a right to be wrong. Before long, however, doubts begin to creep in, and I find myself running through the whole story once again.

It all began two years ago, while I was still at the University of York. It was the summer vacation, and I was attending a conference on nineteenth-century literature at southern university. I should have been looking forward to it, since the nineteenth century is my own particular field, but I couldn't help feeling slightly nervous as I walked across the campus for the first evening reception, mindful that even the best conferences could be a little edgy and awkward at first. On approaching the reception building, I could see that the bar was on a raised terrace looking out over a large artificial lake, and that there was already a gaggle of delegates on the flagstones outside. I walked slowly up the steps to join them. At the top of the stairs there was a young woman who was standing alone and looking about her, as if waiting for a friend. Glancing around the terrace, I saw that none of the people I knew had arrived yet either, and so I stood there for a moment, uncertain what to do. All this time the woman continued to stand before me, pale and pretty, with short blonde hair, a fellow singleton seemingly at a loose end. Perhaps I was feeling altruistic, and wanted to rescue her; perhaps my motives were more selfish, and I was only interested in rescuing myself. Possibly I was genuinely attracted to her, in a way that it is now very difficult for me either to recall or relate. Whatever the motive, whatever the content of my desire, it resulted in a single, unequivocal action: I walked over and introduced myself.

The woman's name was Lucy, and she seemed friendly enough, but as the conversation developed, and I offered to buy her a drink, I couldn't help noticing something slightly nervous and detached in her manner, as if her thoughts were elsewhere. I asked if she was waiting for someone, a friend perhaps.

'Oh no,' she said. 'That is, I did have a friend – my best friend Karen. The plan was that we would come to this, our first conference, together. But a couple of weeks ago she was killed in a car accident. It has been the most terrible shock.'

'Oh God,' I said, 'how appalling. I am so sorry.'

'At first I didn't know what to do. After the accident I hated the idea of coming here on my own. Then I told myself that it is what she would have wanted. So here I am.'

This bombshell exploded the formal distance between us; it was, as Elizabeth Bowen says of the first meeting of Robert and Stella in her Blitz novel *The Heat of the Day* 'the demolition of an entire moment'. I offered to buy Lucy a drink, and as we went up to the bar together, she talked about her friendship with Karen and the fervent academic ambitions they had both shared. Then she gave me a brief description of her thesis, which was a study of nineteenth-century melodrama. Looking at her, I was surprised that she had reached the PhD stage already, because to me at least she still had the fearful, slightly fragile look of a much younger person.

Slowly but surely, round about me, some of the people I knew started drifting into the bar. I introduced her to a couple of them, and then got buttonholed by someone else.

Some time later, I caught a glimpse of her on the other side of the room. She was talking and laughing in a medium-sized group of people, and seemed, on the whole, to be enjoying herself. Suddenly it struck me that, in introducing myself to her a couple of hours before, I had perhaps performed something of a good deed, helping her to negotiate a potentially difficult rite of passage by going over and breaking the ice. And yet, witnessing the speed with which she had thrown herself into the swing of things, it did also occur to me that, probably, she was not nearly as shy or vulnerable as she looked, and would have coped perfectly well without my dubious act of chivalry.

Lucy and I didn't spend a great deal of time together in the next few days, but we were often in the same company, and remained on friendly terms. Like everyone else, we exchanged e-mail addresses on the final day, and I remember stuffing the bit of paper she gave me into one of my jacket pockets, along with countless other scraps and handouts, and a dog-eared sheaf of notes.

We embarked upon a limited correspondence in the autumn, the main purpose of which was to find out whether I would be interested in coming up to her home university to give a seminar paper the following spring. The tone of her e-mails was serious, on the whole: she represented herself as an extremely hard-working and ambitious young woman, desperate to finish her thesis and move on to the next stage of her career. On occasion, however, she would take time out to tease me, toying with the idea that I must be leading a wicked bachelor life. I didn't take this gentle ribbing too seriously, but I did try, equally gently, to defend myself from the charge. 'Really', I said, 'you have no idea. It's not like that at all.'

Early in the following year I decided to apply for a new lectureship that had been advertised at UCL, and ended up being too busy with the application to keep my seminar date with Lucy. Months passed. Having been lucky enough to land the job, I spent the best part of June and July ranging around London searching for a flat. In between jobs, and with plenty of time on my hands, I found myself swimming in a warm current of solitary reverie, strolling the streets until late. With increasing enthusiasm, I began to school myself in the historical topography of the Big Smoke – its underlying structure and story – how the medieval street patterns of Finsbury and Clerkenwell give way, as you move west, to the sedate Georgian geometry of Bloomsbury, and how the early nineteenth century is succeeded by the Victorian era as you stride down Piccadilly towards South Kensington. Even better than this, of course, were all the wild incongruities and interpolations that complicate this general pattern, the strange new growths and even stranger survivals, the dovetailing together of every century, form and faith.

Above all, London seemed a city in which the psychology of freedom had been given objective form. The first few times I wandered through the central crossroads in the City where the Mansion House, the Duke of Wellington's statue, the Bank of England and the Royal Exchange all meet, I thought it a very dull set-piece, a little huddled hub, not a patch on the great public spaces in Paris. Only gradually did I notice the extraordinary dynamism of this very English jumble: the streets branching out from its centre, Catherine-wheeling in all directions, a perfect figure for the tentacled spread of commerce. The very inconsistency of London, with periods and architectural styles continually interrupting and contradicting one another, as if in chaotic family argument, only contributed to this effect. Like the imaginary prisons of Piranesi, the city appeared a strange paradox of liberty in confinement – innumerable stairs and walkways, balconies and arches, great congested avenues and sinuous, serpentine alleyways – all leading everywhere and nowhere, with the beautiful, baffled logic of a dream. My heart was pulled in every direction by these distant objects: I turned and turned again.

It was a good summer, that first summer. By August, I had bought a flat in Spitalfields, which is on the border separating the high-backed beauty of the City of London from the more shabby and stooped appeal of the East End. I still didn't know many people in the metropolis, but I had started to get my bearings, working in the British Library during the week and then continuing my urban explorations at weekends. Only towards the end of September did I begin to feel a little lonely, and start wishing that I had someone else, another greenhorn preferably, to entertain and show around. Then suddenly, out of the blue, I got an e-mail from Lucy. She sounded frustrated with graduate life in the provinces, and said she was thinking of moving to London herself. Spontaneously, I invited her to come down and visit me, sometime before the beginning of term.

Waiting by the barrier at Euston Station on that Saturday morning in early October, I caught an early glimpse of Lucy as she got off the train. There was a purposeful air about her as she took her suitcase down from the carriage and started walking down the platform. She had a red jacket on, as I recollect, and beneath that a black shirt, a short black skirt and a pair of dark red, knee-length leather boots. Ridiculously, I felt a vague sense of anxiety when I saw her striding slowly and deliberately up the platform in those red boots, for they made her seem even younger and more vulnerable than I had remembered, and yet also, in some strange way, more provocative and forbidding.

Inevitably, she and I were both a little wary of one another at first, as was quite natural given that we hadn't seen one another for over a year. Nevertheless, it did strike me as odd that, by late Saturday afternoon, we had still failed to develop much of a rapport. Lucy's talk was full of the frustrations of graduate existence, and I was genuinely sympathetic to her various complaints. The story was only too familiar: she was very impatient to finish her thesis, but felt she wasn't getting nearly enough input from her supervisor, and to make matters worse, there were very few like-minded graduates on campus with whom she could socialise. In between these light laments, we visited some of the sites of central London: Tate Modern, the Soane Museum, Regent Street, St. James's. The day took on a slightly dutiful quality. It's not that I was having a bad time exactly, but almost in spite of myself I did start to think of her visit in terms of an act of generosity on my part, another good turn.

It was over an early evening drink in Gordon's on Villiers Street, surrounded by dark brickwork and waxy bottles, that Lucy told me of another reason why she was anxious to get away from her home campus. She was being harassed, she told me, by a former friend, a man who had become romantically obsessed by her, and was constantly plaguing her with invitations and demands. It didn't seem to matter how many times she told him she wasn't interested, or how often he agreed to remain solely her friend, within a short while he would forget his former resolutions, and resume his campaign. Listening to this story and sipping my wine, I grew noisily indignant on her behalf, and asked her why she did not break off contact, once and for all. She shook her head and told me that it was not as simple as that, for they were both part of the same social group, and it was impossible for her to avoid him as long as she lived in that town.

We stayed for another drink at Gordon's, and yet there was still a curious lack of ease in our manner; indeed by the time we had started looking for a restaurant, I was beginning to wonder whether we were going to run out of things to say. Curiously enough, just as the conversation was drying up, the heavens opened, and we found ourselves skipping across Oxford Street and into Fitzrovia in a heavy shower of rain. There was a patter and swish all about us; water was cascading down the drainpipes and high-kicking along the neon signs; little shimmers of light darted to and fro underneath our feet. I looked down Charlotte Street delighted: the streets were paved with gold. At last, we lighted upon a Thai place at the corner of Charlotte and Goodge Street, and the waiter gave us a table by the window looking out on the Fitzroy Arms. Our menus arrived, and we had just begun to look through them when Lucy laid hers aside, paused for a moment, and then said, quite coolly and deliberately, 'There is something that I have to tell you.'

I looked up. There was an odd tone in her voice. Whatever it was, I knew that it would have nothing to do with nut allergies, or an aversion to white rice.

'I have been in love with you for over a year,' she said. 'It has been such a long time.'

There was something so abrupt and formal about this declaration that I was completely taken aback. I felt like laughing, but couldn't. I hardly knew what to say.

'I am sorry,' she said, 'probably I shouldn't have said that. And now I have spoiled the entire evening.' Her manner was distant, strange. It might have been extreme nervousness on her part, but it came across as a kind of amused detachment, as if she herself were not in any way implicated by what she had just said.

The important thing, or so I thought, was not to make her feel uncomfortable, and so I started to babble, running through a whole series of explanations and excuses in order to fill the silence. I embarked on a long description of a passionate relationship I had had in the past with a woman her age. I talked about all sorts of things just to try and make the atmosphere seem a bit more real. Finally I got round to informing her that I was sorry but it was quite impossible for me to return her feelings: she was too young.

We shouldn't feel the need to supply a reason for not

being in love, but we always do. It is a demand others impose upon us, it is a demand we make on ourselves, and it is a demand we inflict upon our own distant beloveds when they feel forced to turn us down. The fact remains, however, that such things are not subject to explanation, for love, like belief, is neither rational nor voluntary. All we can do is accept, or fail to accept, the excuses that we are given. Lucy failed to accept mine. Of all my shaky reasoning, she appeared immovably sceptical. Somehow or other, I had failed to convince.

Over coffee, I showered Lucy with reassurances that she should not be embarrassed about what she had said, and insisted that, of course, we could still be friends. Inevitably, though, this sudden declaration did colour the rest of her visit. That night my flat didn't seem quite big enough for both of us, and the conversation at breakfast was awkward at best. Rather unnervingly, she had begun to develop a kind of brittle crackle, a sort of hairline fracture, in her voice, which made it seem as if she were always just about to break into some new and more aggressive register, hitherto unheard. I can't remember whether it was the result of a considered attempt to clear up any residual ambiguity between us, or the simple need to flee from this chilly love of hers, but I said goodbye to her a little earlier than expected the following morning. On waving her off at Angel station, I felt immediately relieved. At last I was free of that disapproving gaze. Still, it pained me to think that Lucy might feel humiliated about what had happened. It is not easy to forgive those who have punctured one's pride.

A few days later, she sent me a card. It was a simple thank-you, accompanied by a short note. The next communication, which came a week or so after that, was a good deal longer, and the cheery tone had gone. She had been thinking about our restaurant conversation, she said, and had become increasingly dissatisfied by the explanations I had given. It was ridiculous for me to reject her just because she was a few years younger than I was. What was she supposed to make of an excuse like that? It was time for me to look to my motives: why had I invited her to spend the weekend with me in the first place? What had I been after?

I wrote back to explain myself. It is not easy to tell somebody that you have never had any romantic interest in them, and so I tried to make the point as gently and indirectly as I could, hoping that she would take the hint. The following week she sent me another, far angrier letter, in which she accused me of being a fickle and cold manipulator, a games player who had been deliberately stringing her along. On reading this through for the first time, it was my turn to feel outraged, for I knew perfectly well that such a motive had never been mine. But within a day or so, this anger had begun to nauseate me; I felt degraded and corrupted by it, and became increasingly impatient to transform it into something else. So I started trying to see things from Lucy's point of view. She had misread the situation, certainly, but maybe that had been partly my fault. I tried to think of all the ways in which I might have left things too open, behaved ambiguously; I did everything I could to stifle my wrath.

Another week went by, and I still hadn't made up my mind whether or not to reply to her second letter. Then one afternoon I was coming back to my office after a brief trip to Waterstone's, when I came across Lucy in the corridor, waiting outside my door. She had a defiant look in her eyes. 'Where have you been?' she asked me. 'Nobody knew where you were.' No sooner did I catch sight of her than I felt my pulse quicken and my legs go numb; fumbling for my key, I opened the door and let her in. I was giddy with fear. She had come down to London, she said, in order to visit the library, but also to sort things out between us, once and for all. There was a nervous quiver in her voice. 'This situation can't be allowed to continue,' she said, 'it is too difficult, too upsetting. I need to understand what it is that you want from me. I have to know what this is all about.'

I don't find it easy to lose my temper; the privilege of conducting an angry outburst is something I hardly ever feel. But I did succeed in being extremely curt with Lucy on this occasion, swiftly dismissing her claims. Five minutes later, I sent her on her way – but out of necessity rather than choice. There was an important meeting that I had to go to, and so I had no option but to bring our confrontation to a close. Even at the time, however, it seemed a little cruel to be packing her off so soon; so much so, indeed, it gave me an acute twinge of pain when I imagined her walking disconsolately back to Euston and getting on the train.

She wrote to me again a few days later. In her letter, she said that whatever residual feelings she might have had for me had been completely extinguished by our meeting, for it had revealed a cruel and ugly side to my character, which she now regarded with contempt. A couple of weeks passed. Then another letter arrived. This time it had an apology contained within it – and a sober appeal that at some point in the future we might be able to resume as friends. I felt no sense of triumph on receiving this letter – but rather an enormous sense of relief. I couldn't bear to think of our connection, however brief, as a waste, a failure, a dead blank. It haunted me to think of our relationship – of any relationship – in this way. So I was only too pleased that we had been able to redeem our mutual anger, and salvage something from the wreck.

Gladly, I offered her my friendship once again. It was

a sincere offer, or at least I think it was, but it was also a relatively easy one to make, because such was the geographical distance between us that I didn't imagine our paths would cross very much. Two months later, however, sometime in February, my bluff was called. She sent me a dinner invitation from an address in Hackney, just a few miles up the road. Not only had she moved to London in the meantime, she had also taken a flat in the East End. Of course, it was preposterous to imagine that she had moved to this part of London because of me. Or was it? I felt a faint ripple of fear running through me, which I strove hard to repress. Finally, and despite some considerable misgivings, I decided that the best thing to do was to transform the dinner invitation into a group evening in Soho, and introduce her to a number of graduate students of her own age.

The evening came and went pleasantly enough. The plan was that, by meeting up with Lucy in a group, I could be sociable and yet also maintain a degree of distance, ensuring that, this time, there would be no way that she could get the wrong idea. It seemed a highly successful strategy at the time. Only the following day, in conversation with one or two of the people who had been present, did I really begin to feel uneasy. It seemed that Lucy had spent a lot of time talking about me during the course of the evening, generally in order to criticise various aspects of my character. She had also criticised me for not realising how well suited we were. Then the following day, the second day after our evening in Soho, she sent me another invitation to come to dinner. Now I definitely had a problem. Strictly speaking, of course, she had still done nothing wrong, and there was still no concrete basis to my anxieties, and yet I couldn't help feeling that there was something importunate, even obsessive, about her continuing level of interest. That said, I hated the idea of rejecting her all over again. Like me, she was a new arrival in the big city, and perhaps she had only been trying to be friendly, after all.

Finally, I felt that I was going to have to tell Lucy that I didn't think we were on the right footing for a friendship, and to this end, I decided that the best thing would be to explain this to her gently, over the phone. I was afraid of her, there was no doubt about it, and I didn't want to do anything that would rekindle her rage. Needless to say, however, when I put forward my position, she grew incandescent with anger. A rather savage letter followed. The sole purpose of the Soho evening, she now realised, had simply been to gather incriminating evidence against her, evidence that had been cooked up out of nothing to feed my pathetic self-obsession. I was a paranoid narcissist, she told me. What I couldn't accept – what I didn't want to accept – is that she had long ceased to harbour any romantic feelings for me.

What she couldn't accept – what she found absolutely outrageous in fact – was the appalling manner in which I had treated one of my so-called 'friends'.

Time passed, and the silence grew between us once again. Gradually, the bad memories began to recede. Three months later, sometime in June, I received another text message from her, out of the blue. It was a little note congratulating me on a recent review. The note was generous and well meant – clearly a kind of peace offering – but even though I was quite pleased to receive it, I didn't think it prudent to respond. Then I noticed her name on the list of delegates to the next conference I was attending, which was due to take place in Bristol in three weeks' time. It was inevitable that we should bump into one another on this occasion, and I still hated the idea of there being any continuing unpleasantness between us, and so, after mulling the matter over a little, I finally decided to hazard a reply. Leaving a message on Lucy's answerphone, I thanked her for her text, pointed out the conference coincidence, and then concluded by making a tentative suggestion that we might meet up during the proceedings and have a drink. Shortly afterwards I received another text-message by way of a reply. It contained just one word: INTERESTING. At first, I thought I knew what she meant, but the more I lingered over that bland word on that blank screen, the less certain I felt. The word itself resonated with interest, was deep with her inter-est, and it seemed to get deeper and deeper the longer I looked. Further messages from Lucy followed over the next few weeks – a few too many perhaps. Still, I couldn't quite believe that there was any more mileage to our misunder-standing. Surely it was impossible that this thing would start up all over again.

I couldn't go to the conference in the end: my mother fell sick, and I had to cancel my trip at the last moment in order to visit her. Within hours of my non-arrival, Lucy had already fired off some texts. Where was I? Why had I cancelled? Had I ever had any serious intention of coming at all? And what about the drink I had promised her? When was that going to happen? For once, I felt thoroughly vindicated – and sent a short text explaining my absence. She apologised – and suggested that we should meet up for a drink in London when I got back. This time I didn't reply – meeting up in the city was not what I had had in mind at all. And besides, my mobile phone was on the blink, so I was going to have to take it to the menders before I could respond in kind.

Three days later I was back on the network again, and when I switched my phone back on, a flurry of belated texts bubbled up one after another onto the screen. Every one of them was from her. As soon as she had got back to London she had sought to take me up on my offer. Her first message had suggested a meeting on the Wednesday following the conference, then there had been a second one reminding me of the place and time. The third and fourth, which had been sent on the Wednesday night itself, were angry bulletins scolding me for having failed to turn up at the pub in question. THANK YOU FOR WASTING MY EVENING, she wrote, I HAVE BEEN WAITING HERE FOR OVER TWO HOURS. It was at this moment, I think, that I began to get really worried, for it was clear that I had become trapped in a relationship in which there seemed no way of not being involved.

From that point on, I resolved never to reply to any more of her messages, for I had learned my lesson – at last. But this silent resolution coincided with an equal and opposite decision on Lucy's part, which was to petition me more strongly than ever. Her first letter was bristling with resentment. She told me that she had been so shocked when I had responded to her initial text message that she was physically unable to pick up the phone. 'To be honest I was, at first, incredibly insulted,' she told me. 'After all you had said to me after that night in Soho, all the horrifically inaccurate and hurtful accusations you had levelled at me, you were now, actually, actively ringing me and even suggesting that we have a drink, so pleased were you that I had been in touch. Naturally, I was terribly confused by this incredible reaction from you.' What is more, she said, the messages she had sent me after the conference were prompted solely by a friendly concern for my mother, and that it had been incredibly rude of me not to reply. Gradually however, her messages began to mix anger and appeal; she even sent me a couple of jokey e-mails behaving as if nothing was wrong. And yet whatever the tone of the letters she sent me, it was clear that I must never reply – for I knew now that there was nothing I could say that might not be remoulded, in the forge of Lucy's imagination, into an act of aggression – or desire.

That said, there was no prospect of my being able to detach myself from her letters either; I had to keep an eye on what was happening, just in case things took a turn for the worse. Much of the time, I found myself worrying lest the situation should escalate into some wild accusation or act of violence; on occasion, however, my preoccupations were of a less practical kind. I was still trying to sift through the rights and wrongs of what had taken place between us, and attempting to establish its underlying cause. The few friends I talked to were all in no doubt that Lucy was the one to blame, but somehow this universal consensus only made me question myself more. It struck me as extraordinary that two people in the communication business – for Lucy and I were, above all, language specialists, people who made our living by reading (and talking to) others – should have so spectacularly failed to understand one another, over and over again. Above and beyond the pain that this had caused, I had started to become slightly obsessed by this failure, not least because it called all my critical skills, all my interpretative abilities, into question. Lucy had come to seem like the most difficult of literary texts, somebody so ambiguous as to be almost unreadable, and in the great gaping absence where critical confidence ought to have been, all kinds of guilt feelings rushed in to fill the space.

I ran through her angry questions in my mind: why had I invited her down to London in the first place? Why had I tempted her into making that initial declaration of love only to humiliate her by immediately turning her down? When we met once more, months later, on that group evening in Soho, why had I found it necessary to phone her up a few days afterwards and reject her all over again? And then again, before the Bristol conference, why had I repeated my former behaviour, making a seemingly friendly response followed by a cowardly retreat? What was it, precisely, that she had done wrong? 'If this is a game,' she told me, 'only one of us knows the rules.'

And this silence of mine – and these cowardly retreats: what had I been I afraid of exactly? Was it really violence, or some kind of scandal? Or was it, in truth, her loneliness that frightened me, the very quality that had made me so sympathetic at our first meeting two years ago? In her letters, she told me that she had been talking to distant acquaintances of mine up and down the country, and that all of their stories matched hers: I was an unscrupulous, fickle creature, who had sacrificed romance and even friendship for the sake of being popular. 'There are others,' she wrote, 'who have been clung to only so far as was necessary to feed your ego and your gaping insecurities. You are wholly incapable of sustaining a meaningful union with anyone.'

The worst thing about statements like this was that, even if they hadn't been true when Lucy started writing to me, now they were starting to become so. I was becoming increasingly terrified by the potential claims of others, by the outrageously heavy demands that I felt they were always about to make. I was also becoming obsessed by the possibility that, even in the most anodyne of social conversations, one was always in danger of encouraging intimacies that one had no intention of satisfying, or making inadvertent promises that one would never be able to meet. So with each passing week I withdrew deeper into myself, and Lucy's statements, although she had no way of knowing it, started to take on a kind of prophetic status: 'Your behaviour is not normal,' she would tell me, 'and I fear that one day you are going to end up a very lonely guy.' Invariably, at the end of her letters, she would attempt some kind of rapprochement. 'Deep down', she said, 'we have a lot of things in common. I am not sure if this is what scares you.'

Bombarded by such messages, I began to realise, almost for the first time, what it must be like to be a woman, continually being made responsible for other people's desires. All those attentions to be received and responded to; all those advances for which one will always, no matter how one behaves, end up receiving the blame. No wonder so many women are suspicious. No wonder they become tired of having their fate held in somebody else's hands. I was reminded of the middle-aged heroine in Jean Rhys's *Good Morning Midnight*: 'The lid of the coffin shut down with a bang. Now I no longer wished to be loved, beautiful, happy or successful. I wanted one thing and one thing only – to be left alone.'

Even in Lucy's case, despite her comparative youth, it seemed that obsessive male attention had already been a problem. I remembered the conversation we had had on that day in London, when she told me of the man back at her home university who would not leave her alone. Now, months later, it was as if she had started to see me in the same light. The fact that I was no longer responding to her messages didn't seem to interfere with this interpretation, for from her point of view my non-communication was not a means of disengagement but only a more subtle form of pursuit.

Once, during our confrontation the previous autumn, I had tried to suggest that her experiences with certain men might have affected her attitude to others, but she had been extremely resistant to this idea, saying: 'Do you think of me as a victim? I sincerely hope not.' Despite this, however, there was something in one of her September letters that had set me thinking once again. After running through her usual criticisms, she had concluded, as was her habit, by offering me an olive branch in her final paragraph, adding her home and mobile numbers at the bottom of the page in case I wanted to get in touch. Only at the last minute did she point out that it would not be possible for her to respond directly. She said that she was being dogged by an anonymous caller and I would have to leave a message if I wanted to shout obscenities down the phone.

Perhaps this caller was a crank; perhaps he was one of her new London friends; at all events he was presumably a different man from the one who had been harassing her before. The news worried but did not surprise me. I could imagine all too easily how it might have come about. Lucy was in her mid-twenties, possibly twenty-six or twenty-seven, but she still looked like a young girl. Pale and attractive, with reddish blonde hair, she still had something of the openness, one might even call it the blandness, of youth. Yet behind this girlish appearance there was the guarded manner of someone only too used to being treated as a blank screen for male projections, only too familiar with the Pygmalion gaze. Perhaps that is why she persisted in confusing me with her pursuers, why she kept seeing aggressive desire in every gesture – or non-gesture – that I made. I was older than she was, and one rung further up the career ladder. Perhaps her interest in me had never been anything but a species of professional ambition, a desperate longing to enter into a new sphere of life, where she would finally be able to free herself from a clutch of aggressively unrequited – and undesirable – men.

Sometimes it was her anger that pursued me, sometimes her pain. From the beginning of October, I started to hallucinate her everywhere. When I went to give a paper in Oxford, I thought I saw her walking away from the railway station just as I arrived. She was laughing and joking with another girl, and I became convinced she was going to turn up to my seminar and make a scene. A couple of weeks later, as I was walking through Spitalfields, I thought I glimpsed her standing outside a bar on the other side of the street, looking blank and alone. To walk past in such circumstances, even though I couldn't be sure it was her, felt like a criminal action. Even at such a distance, and in the flickering lamplight of uncertainty, she still had the power to call me to task.

On one level, of course, I knew that nothing I had done to Lucy could warrant such visitations; and yet she kept on reappearing, in my mind and before my eyes, like an avenging angel. The question arose, then, what did she represent? Who or what was the real source of my guilt? Perhaps it was all about sociability, and the breaking of promises too casually made. Perhaps it was a more specific problem.

More than ever, my relation to the opposite sex seemed fraught and uncertain; since Lucy had started writing her angry letters to me, sexuality had come to seem like a particularly terrifying gap. With increasing regularity, I found myself thinking about my past loves, which comprised a couple of long-term relationships, and then a six-month romance. Why hadn't they worked out? Why had I not been capable of making the ultimate commitment? What was wrong with me, I asked myself: was it that I felt too little the proper claims of women – or that I felt them too much?

At night, I had begun to be afflicted by a recurring dream: I was standing before a tribunal, protesting my innocence, defending my cause, and everybody, including the judge, seemed to be solidly on my side. And yet, as the proceedings started to unfold, I alone started to develop a nagging sense that my past history, a history which had, until recently, no particular form or pattern, was now nothing but a long list of guilty deeds.

II

A couple of weeks later I was still receiving Lucy's messages when I arranged to meet up with one of my new friends, a man called Gabriel, in one of the pubs in Soho. He had suggested that we go to the French House on Dean Street, but the little bar was so busy that we decided to take our drinks out onto the street.

It was a warm evening in late October. We were leaning on the sill of the front window, looking out towards the people promenading down Old Compton Street, and then glancing back, every so often, at the medley of cigarettes, hands and glasses just visible under the half-open sash.

'How's your love-life?' I asked. It was a kind of standing joke between us.

'Not great,' he replied. 'Last night I dreamt I was chatting up Death at a party, and my only thought when I woke up was that I had forgotten to get her number.'

'You're making me jealous.' I said. 'Was she nice, Death?'

'Not as stand-offish as you might think.'

'Do you remember Joy, the Chicago girl that I met in the bar at the top of the Hilton?'

'God, she was tough,' said Gabriel, 'she must have spent her entire life grating on that particular expectation.'

'It's a natural reaction,' I said, feeling a brilliant thought suddenly swell into being. 'All Christian names are clumsy prophecies cooked up by our parents, so it's not surprising that so many of us rebel against them. That's why all Veritys are pathological liars, and you can never trust a girl called Faith.'

Gabriel seemed unimpressed. 'What does Gregory mean?' he said.

'Vigilant. Perfect for a half-blind bookworm like myself. Gregory is a name for popes, and for priests who later turn out to be rapists – Rasputin was a Gregory. Whereas I seem to remember that you, Gabriel, are one of the angels.'

'That's funny. Somebody else said that to me recently.'

'Oh really?'

He looked grave. 'It was a woman I got talking to at the British Library,' he said, 'sometime during that last sunny spell. She and I had a couple of long conversations out in the piazza. We talked about life, and about loneliness. On both occasions, she wept. Since then she has been sending me ten, sometimes twenty e-mails a day, convinced that I am her guardian angel, and lying in wait for me on the library steps. I have tried fending her off gently, but it doesn't seem to work. All that happens is that she apologises, get upset, and then declares herself even more strongly than before. I can't bear to be unkind to her, so I have been keeping away from the library lately, working at home. It's a bit difficult, actually, because I really need the books, but I can't wade through all that stuff every morning just to get to the Rare Books room.'

The light was thickening on Dean Street. Throughout Soho the bars and restaurants were getting busy. Lots of people were drinking, chattering, ordering food. Others, sitting in window seats or at pavement tables, were creatures of a different appetite, lending eager, long-lashed looks to the passers-by. I took a gulp of beer. 'But the e-mails she sends – they're never threatening or nasty?'

'Oh no,' he said, 'Just passionate and sad.'

I talked about the messages I had been receiving, and my feelings of guilt.

'A few years ago', said Gabriel, 'a lawyer friend of mine called Jasper defended a woman who had been charged with shoplifting, and she was so pleased when he got her acquitted that she sent him a long, lingering thank-you letter and a big present. More letters followed, and more presents. More expensive presents. Before long she was calling his home. On one occasion, she even followed him and his girlfriend on a motorway trip to the West country, phoning him up every ten minutes from the car behind saying "We need to talk!" In the end, he had to change all his numbers and move to a new flat, partly because he wanted to be free from her romantic attentions, but mainly because he didn't relish being cited in some future prosecution as a receiver of stolen goods. It's an allegory of stalking, in a way; an example of how stalkers turn their victims into accomplices, making them party to the same crime. Meet someone, talk to them, establish a connection of some kind, and before you know it that connection is being used as an unwritten contract, an inadvertent sanction for whatever they have in mind.'

Over dinner that evening in the Café Bohème we got talking to two women seated at the next table. They both worked for Warner Brothers, and their jobs involved looking after Hollywood movie stars when they came over to London. Only the previous week they had been entertaining George Clooney and Brad Pitt.

'Really, they were just ordinary guys,' said Alex, the younger of the two, her dark eyes flashing like a pair of cameras on Oscars night, 'nothing special.'

Slowly but surely the conversation shifted to stalking; first celebrity stalking, then the other kind. To Alex the topic was not nearly as new or intriguing as it had been for me.

'My mother', she said, 'was stalked by her ex-partner for the best part of a year. He followed her everywhere; her only defence was to try and make herself invisible. Every night she would crawl to bed in the dark because she knew he would be watching her bedroom window from the other side of the street. On one occasion she and I were forced to hide in one of the compartments of the bathroom when we heard him walking around downstairs. He was arrested in the end, and sentenced to two years in prison, but he will be coming to the end of his term next year – and we are both very worried about what will happen when he gets out.'

'What can you do?' I asked.

'Well, the new Harassment Law does help a bit,' she said.

Alex couldn't have been much more than about twenty-three, and yet she spoke like a veteran lawyer. Her mother's experience had clearly hardened her, and she had read all the books.

'Under the old law relating to "Loitering with Intent"', she continued, 'stalking victims enjoyed little or no protection. But now they do. Since 1996 any form of intrusive or threatening behaviour repeated over a certain period of time can be punished as an offence, even if the particular behaviour in question is not criminal in itself. The minimum criterion is ten unwanted communications over a period of four weeks.'

I leapt in. 'That's a pretty broad definition, isn't it? I mean, I can see how it would cover the more extreme forms of harassment, but presumably it could also draw many other kinds of behaviour into the same category.'

'Like what?'

'Well – I don't know – like over-friendliness. Bad neighbourliness. Loneliness. Love.'

'What my mother went through wasn't about love,' Alex said, 'but you're right that one of the problems with stalking is that it always lies, to some extent, in the eyes of the beholder. That's why the law defines it as behaviour which any reasonable fellow citizen would agree to be grounds for becoming fearful, referring it to the tribunal of common sense.'

Gabriel told a story about a woman he had known who used to send him strange packages through the post. 'She was very angry with me,' he said, 'for not wanting to go out with her, but the anger took an extremely odd form. Sometimes her packages would have rotting food in them, sometimes a doll's head, sometimes a knife. At the time, I couldn't help thinking of them as threats. I was quite worried, actually; but with the benefit of hindsight I can see that these gestures were figurative, not literal: she was sending me the knife in order not to have to bring it to me by hand. Strange as it might seem, I firmly believe that each package was not a threat but a poem, a work of art.'

Alex and I looked at him, profoundly unconvinced. The other girl, Louise, didn't have any stories of her own to relate. I think she felt a little left out. 'Everybody has a stalker nowadays,' she said, 'except me.'

Strolling home that night down Great Eastern Street I did the usual trick of crossing the road to make clear to the solitary woman walking in front of me that I was not following her, but out of some sudden twitch of curiosity, I gave her a little glance as I did so, and my instant reward, or rather punishment, was to see her look down nervously and quicken her steps.

Suspicious looks in return for ambiguous glances: at what point do the attentions that we give to one another become genuinely disturbing? At what point does the clumsy civility of everyday life, with its innumerable collisions and missed connections, misappropriations and misunderstandings, get transformed into gothic drama? No less importantly, to what extent does our increased awareness of fearful potentialities make fearful stories more likely? I scared the woman on the street almost as much as if I had actually been in pursuit of her: what passed between us, through the medium of the gaze, was nothing so much as the mutual awareness of a possibility, but that was enough to magnetize the distance between us, to transform it into a plot.

The following day I went to the British Library and ordered a number of books on stalking. There were academic studies such as Mullen, Pathé and Purcell's *Stalkers and their Victims*, 'true crime' books such as Richard Gallagher's *I'll Be Watching You* and Gavin de Becker's stalking self-help book *The Gift of Fear*. Broadly speaking, these books were in full agreement as to the nature of stalking. They all defined it as a situation in which one individual imposes on another unwanted and fear-inducing intrusions in the form of communication or approaches. They also concurred on the wide variety of behaviour that was contained by the term. Sometimes, they suggested, the intrusion can be physical, with the stalker behaving like an old-fashioned hunter: tracking, following, laying siege. More often, however, the campaign tends to be waged in a more subtle fashion, via threatening messages or petty vandalism.

Of late, cyberstalking has become increasingly popular: the pursuit of people by e-mail or via the web. Imagining cyberspace to offer some kind of buffer between themselves and their correspondents, many people give away far too much information about themselves when they are on the internet, and then find that apparent physical distance is no guarantee against offensive and intrusive behaviour – not least because it can be dispelled in an instant, once an address or telephone number has been gained. Stalkers don't all want the same thing, the books agreed. Some want love, some revenge. Some are just desperate for a relationship of any kind. In certain cases, the desire to insinuate oneself into somebody else's life is an end in itself; in others it is just the means to an end, which might be anything from the most clinging attachment to violent assault.

Stalkers and their Victims fleshed out the recent history of the phenomenon. Stalking, it pointed out, was a relatively new categorisation of human behaviour, not more than about twenty-five years old. Up until the late 1970s neither the authorities nor the general public had taken it very seriously, invariably considering victims to be in some way complicit with the treatment they received, but gradually, through a number of highly publicised cases of celebrity stalking, most notably those related to John Lennon and Jodie Foster, attitudes had started to change. By the early

1990s stalking began to be thought of as a form of random violence for which the victim bore no responsibility. So too it also began to be recognised that celebrities were not the only people to be stalked. Ten years on, at the turning of the millennium, the authors asserted that the problem had grown considerably, citing a recent study which estimated that every year there were over 200,000 stalkers pursuing their victims in the US alone.

Stalkers and their Victims was also the best source of recent statistics on stalking. Nearly 90% of all stalkers, it said, are male, and the vast majority of their victims – well over 80% – are female. Typically, the offender tends to be an ex-partner or casual acquaintance of the victim (as opposed to a total stranger) and, psychologically speaking, he is likely to be a loner who interacts badly in social situations. Often, he will have experienced a loss or bereavement prior to commencing his intrusive behaviour; or he may have had professional frustrations, such as feeling insecure or under-valued at work. Going further, Mullen, Pathé and Purcell argued that stalkers are often people with frustrated ambitions, aspirational individuals convinced that they were born for better things. Both stalkers and their victims, it was argued, are usually single; and typically they tend to be in their thirties, well-educated, with either professional or semi-professional careers. Much of this sounded eminently plausible – my only problem with it was that it made every ambitious, impatient young singleton in the country sound like a potential stalker. That said, it did intrigue me that stalking was, in many respects, the invention of my generation – the generation that had come to adulthood in the 1990s – the particular craze, as it were, of my sex, age and class. Not that stalkers are always men, of course; the books did make that point. Increasingly it seemed that women are beginning to feel the same bizarre sense of entitlement too. But the vast majority of examples, and certainly the most violent and distressing, were invariably male-on-female, or as the title of Rebecca Gilman's recent play on the subject has described it, *Boy Gets Girl*.

Some psychologists, publishing on the web and in books, have tried to make distinctions between different types of stalker, between the 'love obsessive' who develops a fixation on a person with whom he has no personal relationship, and the 'simple obsessive', who fixes upon a friend, an acquaintance or an ex-partner. Love obsession lumps together people suffering from a serious mental illness, such as acute paranoia or schizophrenia, and people with so-called 'personality disorders', e.g. paranoias of a milder and less debilitating kind. So-called 'simple' obsession is made to cover a variety of different types of behaviour too, from domestic violence cases to *Fatal Attraction*-style fixes. Even within the category of romantic fixation, modern psychology often seeks to distinguish between frustrated lovers who know that they are unrequited, and 'erotomaniacs' who remain convinced, despite all evidence to the contrary, that their love is returned. Indeed, the early twentieth-century French psychologist de Clérambault argued that the term erotomania should be strictly confined to those who believe that they are not active agents in the relationship in question, but merely responding to another's supposed advances. Suggestively enough, with regard to my own situation, Mullen, Pathé and Purcell even went as far as to identify a whole new category of sufferer whom they referred to as the 'false victim of stalking', a person whose hyper-awareness of the stalking phenomenon gives rise to a totally mistaken belief that he or she is being stalked. Despite all these neo-scientific distinctions, however, most of the commentators did accept that there was a lot they did not yet understand about stalking, and that the term itself might cover a multitude of sins.

Ranging more widely in the library catalogue, it became increasingly clear to me that, with the increase in stalking in the last decade, there had been a corresponding growth in stalking literature, from academic sociology to popular self-help books, from Ian McEwan's powerful novel *Enduring Love* to trashy bestsellers and 'true crime'. Two things struck me as a result of my researches. One was that stalking was on the increase. Clearly, reports of celebrity stalking, and of personal harassment among the general population were growing every year. The other was that stalking was encroaching not merely on the street but on the page: with bewildering rapidity, the word had disseminated itself throughout the entire culture. It had made itself ubiquitous, acquiring the status of an umbrella term. Where in the past one might have to search around for the right word to describe a particular dysfunctional relationship, by the late 1990s stalking had become a kind of catch-all phrase. This raised a difficult question: to what extent was the growth in stalking real, and to what extent was it a kind of spectre, a verbal invention, a mere bi-product of popular paranoia? It was not simply that in overusing the word we might be in danger of dumping lots of different kinds of experience into the same narrow plot. It was that at the very heart of this term there might lurk a kind of self-fulfilling prophecy, so that even to think of the stalkerly possibilities in a particular situation might serve to conjure them into being.

Thinking back to my own college days in the late 1980s and early 1990s, I remembered a number of Hollywood harassment films being released at that time, the most notable of which were *Sleeping with the Enemy* and *Fatal Attraction*. Reflecting on them with the benefit of hindsight, it seemed to me that they had helped to publicise the stalking phenomenon, without giving a particularly cogent account of what it entailed. Joseph Ruben's *Sleeping with the Enemy*, which stars Julia Roberts, is all about a woman who fakes her own death in order to escape from her sadistic control freak of a husband, played by Patrick Bergin. The only really gripping bit, as I remember, is when Julia's character, who has been trying to build a new life for herself in a distant town, finally realises that her husband has cottoned on to her whereabouts. The moment of recognition comes when she opens the door of her kitchen cupboard and discovers all the tins standing with their labels facing outwards, perfectly aligned. This was exactly the kind of arrangement that her husband used to insist upon back in their marital home, where he would beat her if either she or the tins ever stepped out of line. This is stalking as a kind of extreme anality, an overmastering obsession with power and control. There is no attempt to explain why Patrick Bergin's character behaves in the way that he does, or why Julia Roberts could ever have thought it a good idea to marry him. Such considerations are beyond the scope of *Sleeping with the Enemy*, whose sole interest lies in the thrill of the chase.

Adrian Lyne's *Fatal Attraction*, which tells the story of a female stalker, is a more intriguing proposition. Early on in the film, the Glenn Close character cites *Madame Butterfly*, that famous paean to the figure of the abandoned woman, as her favourite opera, and true to its masochistic aesthetic, the first thing she does when her lover (who is played by Michael Douglas) shapes up to leave her, is get hold of a kitchen knife and slash her wrists. Michael's character, who is also a *Butterfly* fan, feels genuine sympathy for her distress. He stays a while to comfort her, and to bind up her wounds. By the end of the day, however, he has returned to his wife and family, having told Glenn that their brief fling – which was, in truth, no more than a two-day affair – must come to an end.

It is at this point that Glenn starts to lose her marbles. First she plagues Michael with phone calls, then she vandalises his car, then she sticks his family's pet rabbit in a hot saucepan – the famous 'bunny boiling' scene. Later on, she temporarily kidnaps his daughter, and finally, in a preposterously dramatic dénouement, tries to stab his wife in the bath.

Fatal Attraction is not a great film – but it has imprinted itself quite forcibly upon the popular imagination, and become a kind of touchstone for obsessive female behaviour. The problem with it is not so much that in real life very few women ever resort to violence of this kind, although it is as well to remember this, given the film's continuing prominence in everyone's mind. Rather it has to do with the extraordinary incoherence of the Glenn Close character, for the film functions less as a psychological case-study of an obsessional woman than a kind of mix-and-match source book of stalkerly tendencies, only too clearly a male screen-writer's nightmare-fantasy of female excess. Glenn merely does everything that an independent woman spurned might be deemed capable of doing; she has no specific psychological profile, no particular rationale, of her own. There is no explanation of her sudden switch from *Madame Butterfly*-fancier to variously vengeful harpy. Probably this is because *Fatal Attraction*, in common with so many movies of the late 1980s, is less worried by what a particular woman might get up to than by the phenomenon of go-getting women in general, as is borne out by the final bathroom scene, in which Michael Douglas's wife (played by Anne Archer) is suddenly transformed from the dopiest of home-makers into a slavering homicidal maniac. Notionally, of course, Anne's violence is justified because she is defending her family, but she does so in such a manner that, by the end, it is a moot point which of the two women is the more scary – her or Glenn Close.

There is something very heavy-handed about this. It is as if the director is trying to tell us that all women have extremely violent emotions bubbling away beneath the surface, and that they need to be kept in positions of domesticity and docility in order to be protected from themselves.

In both *Sleeping with the Enemy* and *Fatal Attraction* stalking is depicted as a pathological form of behaviour, at once irrational and extreme. In neither case are the victims in any way responsible for the treatment they receive. So too, in all the books I consulted on the subject, the main purpose, apart from the obvious desire to entertain, was to vindicate the victims, to absolve them of all blame. Stalking, so the books said, was nothing to do with love, and all about power and control. Victims were encouraged to realise that it was an obsessional form of behaviour and should not be taken personally. I wondered about this a little. Broadly speaking, this seemed the right emphasis to make: continual harassment is a terrible violation of another person's security and privacy; nobody deserves to be put upon in this way. The problem was that in falling over themselves to defend the victims of stalking these books were in danger of protesting too much. It seemed that they couldn't cope with the idea that in many cases stalking might be a form of relationship, albeit of the most dysfunctional and destructive kind. So too, in continually insisting upon a clear distinction between normal love and pathological fantasy, they betrayed an underlying anxiety that actually there was no clear dividing line between the two. The more rigidly, in fact, they tried to mark out stalking as a discrete current of human behaviour, the more it seemed to leak into everything else.

One example of this came from *Stalkers and their Victims*, the respectable academic study that I mentioned before. Insightful in many ways, it was also curiously obtuse in others. It argued that stalking was closely linked with many aspects of modern society, but that to some extent it had always been around. Going back to the medieval period, the book cited the Italian poet Dante Alighieri's famous love of Beatrice, as expressed in his verse-autobiography the *Vita Nuova*, as an early example of stalkerly behaviour; indeed it even went as far as to suggest that male romantic obsession might have been *more* common in Dante's time: 'Western society at that period', it argued, 'accepted as an ideal an autistic love constructed by a man out of projections and fantasies that took no account of the realities of the actual woman.' Reading this in my little pew in the British Library, I grew immediately indignant on Dante's behalf. Surely the Cambridge authors had completely missed the point of the *Vita Nuova* and the courtly love tradition out of which it emerged. I lifted my head and looked about me. It was a Saturday. The main reading room had only a thin sprinkling of people. All was calm. It was an odd place to get heated – and yet for some reason I felt a strange urgency about this issue. Going up to the on-line catalogue,

I requested two copies of the *Vita Nuova*, one in English and one in Italian, and also the *Life of Dante* by the poet's near contemporary Giovanni Boccaccio. Having placed my order, I went back to wait in my seat. Had Dante been a stalker? Suddenly it seemed important to find out.

It had been a long time since I had read the *Vita Nuova*, and I had almost forgotten what a spare and simple story it was. Dante first met Beatrice when they were both nine years old. Their meeting took place at a flower festival in their home-town of Florence, the city of flowers, in the year 1274. It was not unusual for people to be struck by Beatrice Portinari, so Boccaccio tells us, for her features were 'so full of beauty and modest grace that she was declared by many to be like a little angel'. On seeing her, Dante felt his heart speak prophetically to him: 'Here is a God stronger than I,' it said, 'who shall come to rule over me.' Nine years later, when the young poet was eighteen, he was formally introduced to her again. She was dressed in pure white, and standing between two ladies of high bearing. It was at this moment, Dante says, that Love truly became his master, and he embarked upon what he called a *vita nuova*, a new life. According to Boccaccio, 'nothing else was pleasure or repose or comfort to him except seeing Beatrice, as if from her face and eyes he would obtain his every happiness and complete consolation.' At first, the young poet tried to keep his passion a secret, diverting suspicion from himself by using another lady – to whom he would write eloquent sonnets and letters of love – as a 'screen of the truth'. Ultimately, however, this plan backfired: rumours of Dante's ill-treatment of this lady caused Beatrice to refuse him greeting in the street, and he retreated into solitude, distraught.

In this solitude, Love appeared to Dante in a dream, urging him to write a poem to his beloved in which he expressed the true condition of his heart. Love also told him that he must not address her directly, for it was only if he kept a respectful distance, and allowed the sweet melody of poetry to intercede for him, that he would deserve to be reprieved. Dante gave up using another woman as a screen to protect Beatrice's reputation, but it is clear that he continued to think the concept of the enabling obstacle a good one, because it remained absolutely central to his idea of love. In personifying Love as a sort of adviser or chaperone, Dante gave it an objective existence, quite distinct from his own selfish desires, and by arguing that love poetry, at its best, should always be in some sense indirect, he went on to suggest that it too, like a kind of intermediary, could be used to intercede between the lover and his beloved, protecting them from one another.

One of the most modern things about the *Vita Nuova* is that Dante never pretends it is easy to sublimate one's passion; the book is full of amorous torment, as the lover moves painfully through the various stages of love. However, it is precisely because of this sense of struggle that the final triumph is so impressive. In this sense, the *Vita Nuova* represents the unrequited love story in its ideal form. Through faith, and through art, the various obstacles and blocks that prevent intimacy between the poet and his beloved in the physical realm provide the occasion, the opportunity even, for what Dante considers to be a more fulfilling 'relationship' at a spiritual level. Poetry becomes an important means not merely for expressing but also for mediating the lover's passion. Feelings of pain and loss, of sickness and wasting, become transmuted as Dante learns how to rejoice in Beatrice as an example of the beautiful, the graceful and the good, and it is by this means that Beatrice herself gradually comes to be seen as a mediating figure in her own right, a go-between drawing Dante closer to God.

Tragically, Beatrice Portinari died when she was only twenty-four years old. This early martyrdom was an absolute catastrophe for Dante the man, but it allowed Dante the poet to reinforce an analogy which had been central to his poetic imagination from the beginning – the figurative link between Beatrice and that other martyr, Jesus Christ. Obsessed, like every other lover, with reading gestures as signs, Dante started interpreting certain details relating to Beatrice's life – numbers, dates, elements of dress and behaviour – as religious indicators, indicators leading through and beyond her to the heart of the Christian gospel.

Does the *Vita Nuova* give a reliable account of Dante's relationship with Beatrice? Boccaccio says it does, noting that 'as Dante himself writes, and as others to whom his desire was known report, his love was most virtuous, and there never appeared, by look or word or sign, any wanton appetite either in the lover or in her whom he loved.' The biographical evidence is so scant, however, that we may never know for sure. It is possible that his obsession with Beatrice did develop into a form of personal harassment, albeit of a rather formal and courtly kind. Such speculations have no bearing on the assessment of the Cambridge editors, however, because it was not independent historical evidence relating to Dante's life that led them to condemn him, but the evidence of the *Vita Nuova* itself – as if it was only too evident from this text alone that Dante's unrequited attachment had been autistic and unhealthy.

This is a very modern judgement. Such is the commitment to the principle of reciprocity in the modern age that any model of love that looks too one-sided, or in which there is too much of an imbalance between the lover and the beloved, is bound to seem dysfunctional. With good reason, we prefer our lovers to be on the same footing as us, and for our love to be paid back in kind. Nor are we comfortable with the model of love-as-service. The language of chivalry makes us suspicious, not least because of the way it has been used, since Dante's time, to marginalise rather than valorise women's social role. Pedestals, we have come to realise, immobilise as well as exalt. We are impatient of mediations and obstacles, whether social or religious, seeing them as artificial and unjust. With the decline of Christianity, and its Platonic tradition in particular, we no longer like to think of our loves as mediations of the ideal. So too, it is less interesting for us to contemplate the little hurdles of love that prevailed between the respectable classes at this time, such as arranged marriages, and the antagonisms between noble families – than to think of the much larger and more impermeable obstacles of wealth and rank that separated these classes from the rest of society. Liberty and equality are our watchwords – liberty because we believe that both men and women should have a free choice of partner, and equality because we believe that relationships should be based on equal rights and mutual respect.

That said, the Cambridge editors may have taken their modern prejudices too far. It is one thing to point out the distant nature of Dante's romance with Beatrice, it is another thing to pathologise it simply on that account. The editors may have been attempting to put a *cordon sanitaire* around romantic love, protecting it from its more rabid relations, but in dismissing all 'projections and fantasies' as 'autistic', I felt that they had effectively thrown baby Cupid out with the *Fatal Attraction* bath water. For what is love, I reasoned, if not a species of imaginative investment, a willingness to see the good in and beyond appearances? It is good to have some knowledge of one's beloved, and to have had some first-hand contact with him or her – but can the absence of such knowledge or contact really disqualify a lover entirely? How many people, I wondered, really know their lovers before they fall in love with them? How many of us can really say that our passions have been grounded on deep familiarity and a thoroughly rational assessment?

The more I thought about it, the more it seemed to me that the editors had been guilty of inflicting their own modern prejudices upon an incident in the past. It was as if they could not imagine a form of distant desire that wasn't, in some way, delusional. What is more, there was an underlying assumption that Dante's passion had been frustrated – i.e. that his main aim had been carnal, and that he had been disappointed in that end. It is one thing to acknowledge the importance, the central significance, of physical desire; it is quite another to assume, as we moderns increasingly tend to do, that it is the only consummation worth considering, and that all romance is essentially driven by the urge to have sex. Dante's vision of love transcended the realm of physical desire. Far from offering a prototype of modern encroachment, the very formal poetry of the *Vita Nuova* offered an object lesson in how to keep one's distance, in how to preserve, even in the midst of the most ardent longing, a strong sense of the mystery and otherness of the beloved.

It is tempting to relate this lack of a sense of distance in relation to the past – the grand assumptions that we moderns increasingly tend to make about the underlying truth of former ages – with the sense of entitlement, the assumption of false intimacy, that is at the heart of stalking. Stalkers are impatient of obstacles: they are always trying to collapse the distance between themselves and the object of their desire. That is why they are often so fond of e-mail, the internet and the mobile phone: they get drawn in by the promise of instant intimacy that the modern media provides. Unlike Dante, they do not like to see things in metaphorical or figurative terms: literal proximity, literal possession – these are the only things that count. Stalkers love the media, but are impatient with mediation. They live in a universe without forms or frames. Hence the celebrity stalker will start harassing the female newsreader because she wishes him goodnight at the end of every evening. He will want to make the weathergirl's promise of warmth come true. What makes matters worse is that, with increasing enthusiasm, television and magazines actually encourage this kind of fantasy. More than ever, they like to tantalise us with our seeming proximity to the rich and famous. Not only are public-voting TV shows such as *Big Brother* and *Pop Stars* cruelly exploitative of their contestants' desire for celebrity, they are also highly manipulative of their audience too, for they thrive on suggesting that there is a real, open and democratic relationship between the people on screen – that is, the presenters and contestants – and the viewers at home. It is not simply that this fake intimacy is voyeuristic and intrusive, it is also dishonest – since what happens on screen is always very carefully edited, packaged and controlled. As TV's capacity to simulate reality becomes ever more convincing, the onus is on us to remember that reality television is not real. Considered in these terms, the likelihood is that the stalking phenomenon has much more in common with our own immediate media than with the *Vita Nuova*'s deferred ideal.

Can one have a truly democratic culture, a culture of equality, without this sense of false entitlement? To an increasing degree, the information society makes us feel that we have an instinctive and immediate purchase on the lives of others. It makes us feel that we know them. But even more worryingly, in a way, it also seems to be generating a growing conviction that we have a kind of innate imaginative property over them, a *right* to know them. With each passing year, we subject more of our fellow citizens to the kind of treatment that used to be reserved for celebrities. We believe that we ought to be able to gain access to anyone.

In conversation about stalking, I was struck by the large number of friends and colleagues who, when asked if they had ever been harassed or pursued by someone else, would start by saying 'Oh no', then think for a moment, correct themselves, and start telling me about an incident from their past. They always seemed to have a story to tell. I knew a number of men, Gabriel among them, who had been targeted at certain points in their lives. One friend had received over a hundred and fifty e-mails from a woman he had met once at a party. But it was only when talking to my female friends that I realised the full extent of the problem. A bewildering number of them had been harassed at one time or another. My experience, it turned out, was just the tip of the iceberg. With these women, it was ex-boyfriends who were the main problem. One ex-girlfriend of mine, with whom I was still in touch, talked eloquently of having been peppered with messages by a former partner. While they were going out together, he had been extremely possessive, and when she eventually called their relationship off, he had refused to let go. Suffused with righteous indignation, his messages were all the more chilling for being so controlled. At random moments in her day, she would look up from her desk, click the flashing envelope on her mobile phone, and text messages such as THANK YOU FOR RUINING MY LIFE would be blurted out onto the screen. Or she would be getting ready to turn in at night, and another little missive would inject itself into the gap between the bathroom and her bed. I DON'T KNOW HOW YOU CAN SLEEP AT NIGHT AFTER WHAT YOU HAVE DONE TO ME.

There was a terrible virtuosity in all this. Through discipline and practice, he had managed to turn the text message form into a little haiku of hate; and because of the nature of the genre, these tiny acts of revenge were perfectly adapted to catch their victim unawares, sliding into the little slips and folds of her life when her guard was down. This campaign lasted some time, but it was combined and then eventually superseded by another equally effective tactic: silence. Five or six times a day he would call her, only to hang up when she answered the phone. Occasionally he would wait until she put back the receiver, or sob a little down the mouthpiece without saying a word; and all too often she found herself hanging upon these empty messages, like a child over an empty well, waiting for something to rise up from the depths. Slowly but surely, a new sound-world was opening up around her, one in which absence was more threatening than presence, and silence an acoustic of fear. Out in the world of day there was no question, at least from her friends' point of view, that she had behaved impeccably: it had been a bad relationship, they all agreed, and she had been right to set herself free. Yet on hearing the ringing, the distant breathing, and then the click and burr of the receiver, her own feelings were very different. This abstract frieze of sounds had a hieroglyphic hold on her. It meant everything because it said nothing. It told her that the price of her freedom had not yet been paid. This soundtrack is coming to serve as a prelude to violence in an increasing number of lives; in her case, however, its threat remained latent, unfulfilled. Nevertheless, her stalker's campaign was still extremely effective in its way, for it did succeed in recruiting her to his cause, training her up to persecute herself.

In its purest form, stalking is not a physical crime like rape or assault, nor is it a mere trailer to such things. It is a species of thought-crime, complete in itself. It turns its victims into paranoid obsessives who hover uncertainly between self-justification and self-reproach. Initially, the stalker's effect on his victim is not wholly negative. The fact that somebody else, a stranger perhaps, has chosen to take such an intense interest in us cannot fail to expand our sense of self. It offers objective confirmation of that secret suspicion of ours that we are, after all, something special. The idea that something out there is interested in us, and is watching carefully how we behave, helps give a new meaning to our actions. It misleads us to thinking of our own life as a significant history, something worth following.

'There is no God,' we might say to ourselves, 'but at least I have my stalker.' Before long, however, the true nature of this interest begins to make itself evident, and what previously seemed a celebration of uniqueness turns into a form of persecution. And the more we are persecuted, the more we ourselves will come to regard individual difference as a criminal quality. We begin to fear that the very things – the very tiny things – that distinguish us from the rest of the world, are precisely those things that the world itself will come to loathe, and spend all our time imagining the infinite number of ways in which we could be despised.

If the victim of stalking can be considered to be suffering from too much identity, the stalker is the one who suffers from too little. That is why so many stalkers chase celebrities. As Gavin de Becker puts it in *The Gift of Fear*, 'in their quest for attention and identity, these people go to the people who have most identity to spare: famous people.' The stalker has a desire to be noticed; he wants his existence confirmed. Sometimes this confirmation is sought solely through acts of punishment. By inflicting suffering, he forces his victim to acknowledge he is there. More often, however, he seeks his confirmation through love. Inevitably, stalkers tend to adopt a rather theological attitude to romance. Each one reads his beloved's gestures like an old-style puritan looking for signs of salvation, poring over every leaf and flower for the confirmation he seeks. That's why he tends to find any ambiguity or indifference in the love object maddening: it leaves a great question mark at the heart of nature. The classic stalker is like Captain Ahab hunting the White Whale, for it is not merely an elusive object that he has set out to track down, but elusiveness itself.

The opposite of stalking is not love. They have far too much in common for that. The opposite of stalking is flirtation – a form of sociability which allows us to entertain the possibility of other people without wanting to fix their meaning. Flirtation opens up a dialogue while continuing to maintain a degree of distance. It is, as Adam Phillips says in his essay on the subject, a way of being promising without making any promises, a means of playing for time. To some people flirtation is cruel, without conviction; but to others it is liberal and tolerant, without a desire to convict. Either way, stalking is at war with this principle, for stalking, in its purest form, wants nothing better than to move in and close the gap. Everything that is indistinct and undecided in our relations with one another, everything that is, in a sense, free, stalking thinks of as a kind of smokescreen, an obstacle to be surmounted, a lie. Stalking is the erotic impulse pushed to the point of principle, with all of its delightful distractions and deferrals, all of its scrupulous fetishism, cast aside. Stalkers are impatient to rush to the end game, with no sense that once you reach the end, the game is up. The problem is that in conceiving passion in such polarised terms – either she loves me completely or she has no feeling at all; either our life will be a heaven together, or I will make hers a hell – they are always narrowing the distance between love and death. Stalkers leave themselves, and their victims, with no room for manoeuvre. They are the fundamentalists of love.

That was why the letters I received from my 'stalker' Lucy succeeded in affecting me so deeply: they appealed to my puritanical side. Like my own conscience, they would not let me get away with anything. The problem was not that they were beyond my sympathy, but that I could sympathise only too well. I knew I had never had any conscious designs upon her – that was not the problem; it was the world of my twilight motives of which I felt afraid. Her interpretation of my behaviour presented me with a vision of sexuality in which every gesture was ambiguous, always tainted by connotations one could not control. By taking everything the wrong way, Lucy succeeded not merely in undermining my social confidence, my ability to predict the kind of effect I might have on others, she also resurrected deep fears of mine that men and women would never be able to communicate with one another properly because of the manner in which sex got in the way. Everyone is condemned to have a sex. It is our original sin. And no matter how creative certain people are in manipulating their gender identity, there is still a pitiful paucity in the number of roles that we are allowed to play. New man, mother superior, seductress, cad: what a narrow repertoire it is, when one comes down to it, and how distressing to throw away one script only to find an even more hackneyed one lying beneath. To my mind at least, relations between the sexes had become so hopelessly bedevilled with confusion and misunderstanding, so hopelessly fraught with multiple little unintended cruelties, that, as in the famous song, I wanted to call the whole thing off. How wonderful it would be, I thought, if this obstacle could be cleared away – if relationships could be as transparent and pure as they had been in one's childhood. This is one of the curious things about stalking – that however unsuccessful stalkers are in their pursuit of their victims, they do often succeed in converting them to their religion. The world of adult sexuality looks dangerous and corrupt after stalking. It brings out the puritan in us all.

Sometimes I would leave an e-mail of Lucy's unopened, and the name and subject would lie there in my inbox, thick with meaning, and yet in the end I would lose my nerve and open it, and her heart would spill out onto the screen. It didn't seem to matter how long it had been since she was last in touch, or what had happened to me in the meantime. Her letters always called me back to the same place and time, cancelling the interval between. It was like being told that one's real life, the life one thought one was living, was actually quite insubstantial and irrelevant. It was like having one's character constantly rewritten by someone else. I thought of that extraordinary story by Stefan Zweig, the *Letter from an Unknown Woman*, which was later made into a film by Max Ophüls. Zweig's story tells of a woman's lifelong love for an older man. She meets him first as a young girl, then as a young woman, and finally as a mature adult. She even fathers a child by him – a little boy – the product of a single night of passion. But because these encounters are so widely spaced and fleeting, he never remembers her from one meeting to the next. A writer and a man about town, he carries on living his life in his own sweet way, and remains utterly oblivious to the central role that he has played in hers. Hence it is a devastating experience for him to read over this dying woman's letter, a last confession that is all the more annihilating because so much of its anger is repressed: 'My boy died yesterday,' she writes. 'Now I have only you left in the world; only you, who do not know me; you, who are enjoying yourself all unheeding, sporting with men and things. Only you, who have never known me, and whom I have never ceased to love.'

A couple of days after my trip to the library, I decided to reply to one of Lucy's e-mails. Risky as it was, I was desperate to bring this phantom narrative to an end – not least because it was beginning to turn me into something of a phantom myself, in constant flight from everyone else. Where Lucy was concerned, however, the aim of writing was not to reach out, but cut myself clear. One cause for hope lay in the fact that, unpredictable and intermittent as her correspondence had been, it had taught me certain important things about her. She was tenacious, certainly, but she was not terrifying. No longer was I half-expecting her to make some wild allegation, or to turn up at my flat with an axe in her hand. 'Please don't flatter yourself that I have any inclination to follow you around,' she had written at one point, 'you are far too unimportant to me for that.'

It was hard composing the letter – not least because I had to suppress my sympathy as well as my anger. I told her that

I did not feel bitter towards her, but that she must stop getting in touch. 'I am not interested in any kind of relationship with you,' I said, 'most people would have got the message by now'. I didn't attempt to address any of her accusations; I didn't even try to give my version of events. I simply said that it was very upsetting to be continually peppered with these declarations and demands, and asked her, once and for all, to stop.

Then a surprising thing happened; a few days later I received a long e-mail from a complete stranger, a woman called Anna. She introduced herself as a close friend of Lucy's, who was replying on her behalf. 'We have never met,' she wrote, 'and thankfully nor are we ever likely to. I am writing to save my friend the bother of this, the final ever correspondence she will ever have with you.' Anna's epistle was a sustained attack on my cruelty and immaturity. It also contained a complete step-by-step vindication of Lucy's behaviour towards me. Anna acknowledged that at times Lucy had demanded correspondence from me, and that I had clearly been discomfited by this, 'However, there her crime ends, and yours surely begins, for if Lucy has read into your messages, then this has surely been your intention from the start.'

Nor did the barrage of letters, as you put it, contain any

declarations of love, they were only demanding redress of the many injustices your arrogance and selfishness have visited upon her. How could a man of thirty-four be so incapable of adult sentiment and behaviour? Have we not all had friends who at some point have declared feelings slightly stronger than our own? Do we then shy away like an embarrassed schoolboy? No, we do not. Conversely, these are the very people who become our closest friends, because whilst that bond may never be love, there is something in those people, and something they value in us, that is worth monopolising upon and preserving. All of this however is of little consequence to me. I take issue only with the fact that you seek to blame your blatant inadequacies on her. If you are too rude to bother, or are simply incapable of sustaining normal human interaction, do not impose the blame for this on her – I will not have a friend of mine mentally tortured in this way.

In conclusion, Anna confirmed that Lucy would never try to contact me again: 'Your snivelling little request will be willingly adhered to,' she said, 'you are not worthy even of her disdain.' I hardly knew what to make of this letter. It contained such a detailed account of what had happened between Lucy and myself that at first I strongly suspected Anna of being a little woolly dolly that Lucy took to bed with her at night; in fact it was only too easy to imagine them whispering across the pillow to one another in their matching pyjamas: 'We think he's horrid, don't we?'

Perhaps Anna was real; perhaps she was nothing but a kind of phantom replacement for the lost figure of Karen, that friend of Lucy's who had died. Either way, Anna's interposition, her mediation one might almost call it, seemed to mark a decisive moment. It was as if, by allowing someone else to express her anger, Lucy had finally managed to get some distance from the situation and set herself free. I couldn't recognise Anna's representation of Lucy as a patient and suffering women, a kind of latter-day Madame Butterfly, but I had to acknowledge its efficacy. It turned Lucy from an unrequited lover into an abandoned woman. No longer was she an active pursuer, a role that she had always strenuously denied; she had metamorphosed into a kind, sincere woman who had been cruelly cast aside. Neither role was particularly rewarding; there was pain and shame in both. Nevertheless, there might be certain benefits, it seemed to me, in choosing to be abandoned; it meant a transformation of oneself from a frustrated subject into a suffering object, a swapping of powerlessness for passivity. It meant the swallowing, or expulsion, of all one's actively destructive feelings. More to the point, it seemed to have helped Lucy achieve what so few men in her position ever seem able to achieve: acceptance.

I never heard from Lucy again. Anna's letter had brought the story to an end, and as I looked back on it, weeks later, with the mists of fear and anxiety slowly dispersing, it all became a little clearer in my mind. It may have been naïve of me, given how little I really knew about her, but I couldn't help thinking of Lucy as a stalking victim, someone for whom desire had become something remote and unforgiving, a relentless pressure from without. Perhaps that was why, in deciding to become fixated upon me, she had been so stubbornly indifferent to rebuffs, for it was possible that she was only pursuing me as she herself had been pursued: coldly, a little contemptuously, and with a sense of complete entitlement. But in the end, of course, I knew that everything I thought about Lucy would have to remain deeply conjectural, for I would never know her well enough to take a more confident line. I could never be certain that she had been damaged by past relationships, the only thing I could be sure of was that she had damaged mine. Fleeing from what I now considered to be the impossible claims of others, I retreated deeper into myself; I wanted nothing to do with love or relationships ever again. Whatever the cause of my disastrous collision with Lucy, the final result was clear: between us we had managed to pathologise romance.

III

On the morning of October 16th 1832, the French writer Stendhal found himself looking out over a glorious prospect. He was standing in dazzling sunshine by the church of San Pietro in Montorio, on the Janiculum Hill in Rome. The entire city lay spread out before him, from the Appian Way, with its ruined tombs and aqueducts, to the beautiful garden of the Pincio recently built by the French. Musing on this distant prospect, he found that against his will ancient Rome prevailed over modern Rome, and memories of Livy began to crowd into his mind. On Monte Albano, to the left of a convent, he could see the fields of Hannibal. 'What a magnificent view!' he said to himself, 'There is no place like this in the world.' Then his thoughts drifted slowly back to his own life and character. 'Ah!' he said to himself, 'in three months' time I will be fifty; can it really be so?' The thought astonished him. He sat down on the steps of the old church to ponder it further. 'I shall soon be fifty,' he sighed, 'it's high time I got to know myself. I should really find it hard to say what I have been and what I am.' It was twilight before Stendhal finally came down from the hill. A light evening mist had finally teased him out of his reverie, forewarning him of the sudden chill that, notoriously in this region, always follows immediately after sunset. Before setting off, however, he made a point of commemorating his day of contemplation at San Pietro by writing '16 octobre 1832, *J. vaisa voir la 5*' on the inside belt of his white English trousers, a thinly disguised version of 'I am going to be 50'.

A few days later, he was walking along a lonely path overlooking the Lake of Albano, still musing on the same question, when he came across a little bench by the side of the road. He stopped to sit down. Thinking back, he knew that, even by the extraordinary standards of the age, his life had been extremely eventful. In 1800, at the age of 17, he had gained a commission in Napoleon's army, and his soldiering duties had taken him to Germany, Switzerland, Italy and Hungary. From 1803 he had spent three years loafing around Paris, living the life of a bohemian student, before returning to the army as an administrative officer in 1806. In the second phase of his military career, he had taken part in the Russian campaign of 1812, witnessing at first hand the disastrous retreat from Moscow, in which thousands of his fellow Frenchmen had perished in the ice and snow. Yet as he stared blankly at the soil beneath his feet, he was suddenly struck by the fact that, varied and colourful as his career as a soldier had been, it did not provide the key to his character. It did not say anything about the kind of man he was. Rather, his life could be summed up by the following names, the initials of which he scratched, one by one, in the dust with his stick:

Virginie
Angela
Adèle
Mélanie
Mina
Alexandrine
Angeline
Angela
Mathilde
Clémentine
Giulia
Mme Azur

It was the list of his past loves. Some were slender infatuations; others grand passions that had rumbled on for years. Virginie and Melanie were actresses; Alexandrine a French countess. Adele was a virtuous Parisian bourgeoise. Angela's father supplied clothes to the French army; Mina's was the military governor of Brunswick. Clémentine was the spouse of a French officer; Mathilde the estranged wife of a Polish one. Madame Azur was a French financier's wife, who later became the mistress of the painter Eugène Delacroix. Giulia was the ward of the Tuscan minister to France. One thing only united these twelve names: the fact that, taken together, they made up the calendar of Stendhal's heart. To catalogue one's past conquests in this way might argue an affinity with Don Giovanni; or even Napoleon, whose spectacular progress had often been summarised in terms of a simple list of names: Marengo, Austerlitz, Jena, Wagram. But Stendhal was not that kind of man. Nor could his romantic life be construed as a string of heroic victories, for he had endured more than his fair share of tear-strewn Waterloos.

In conversation, Stendhal was an extremely charismatic man; and he had a real gift for making friends with elegant, intelligent women, but he had never been attractive or forceful enough to make love to them successfully; hence all of his more ardent sentiments had remained unreturned. He was not a bitter man, however. Having carved his lovers' names in the dust, he reflected that 'most of these charming creatures have never honoured me with their favours, but that, nevertheless, they have literally taken up my whole life.' He saw that he had made a lifetime's career out of being an unhappy lover, and that he had enjoyed daydreaming above all other things. As he tells us in his autobiography, the *Life of Henry Brulard*:

> I was in deep reverie about these names and the astonishing stupidities and follies they made me commit (I mean astonishing to me, not to the reader, and in any case I've no remorse for them). In actual fact, I possessed only six of these women whom I loved.

Everyone knows that our life is so much more than the story – the story we have to keep telling ourselves – of our success. The problem is that our failures are so very difficult to remain faithful to. Unrequited loves are a case in point. However passionate they may have been, the tendency is always to look back upon them with a kind of historical irony, to disavow them as part of some absurd costume drama of the past. They are like the ruined aqueducts running through the prospect of Rome: almost impossible to harmonise with the emotional geography of the present.

Stendhal was committed to thinking well of unrequited love. It may have been the artist in him, always wanting to find something rich in his past experience; it may have had something to do with his Bonapartism, and the deep need, especially in the years immediately after the fall of Napoleon in 1815, to see defeat as just another form of triumph. Significantly, his most passionate love affair dates from the post-Waterloo period. It took place in Italy, where he had sought solace for the fall of empire in opera, good society and Renaissance art. The woman he fell in love with was Mathilde Dembowski, whom he met in Milan in 1818. She was twenty-eight years old, married but separated, a passionate and intelligent woman who was secretly involved in the cause of Italian liberation. Stendhal was to be in love with Mathilde, intensely but unrequitedly, for three long years. It was only in 1821, after having been accused of liberal sympathies by the Austrian authorities and forced to return to Paris, that he finally managed to gain a degree of distance from the affair. While in Paris, he put the finishing touches to a book he had been writing, off and on, during his infatuation with Mathilde. It was a collection of reflections and anecdotes dressed up to look like a scientific treatise. The title was simply *On Love*.

Partly, *On Love* is Stendhal's attempt to cure himself of his passion for Mathilde, hence the mock-scientific tone;

but it is also, no less obviously, a heartfelt defence of romantic love as a source of pleasure, not least love of the unrequited kind. Describing the manner in which love takes root in the individual subject, Stendhal likens it to the way in which, if you place a tree branch in one of the mines at Salzburg and leave it there for a couple of weeks, gradually salt crystals will grow over the entire exposed area, leaving no vestige of the original branch beneath. A person in love, Stendhal says, crystallises about his or her beloved in exactly the same way, by making the beloved a focus for diverse pleasing associations and impressions, all of them retrospective justifications of a choice that has already been made.

Stendhal gives us a number of examples of the crazy logic of crystallisation. Imagine you are in love, he tells us. One day a friend of yours goes hunting and breaks his arm. Suddenly you think to yourself, quite out of the blue: 'Wouldn't it be wonderful to be looked after by the woman you love!'

To be with her all the time and to see her loving you... a broken arm would be heaven... and so your friend's injury provides you with concluding proof of the angelic kindness of your mistress. In short, no sooner do you think of a virtue than you detect it in your beloved.

Because the work of love is essentially imaginative, it needs time to develop and grow. Hence the best romances are those that move forward gradually, in Stendhal's opinion, because it is only through a long process of crystallisation that the lover's investment in the beloved will become fixed and secure. To this end, Stendhal professes himself a devoted admirer of female modesty, because, as he says repeatedly, romance would not be possible without it. Women's pride puts obstacles in the way of romantic desire in both sexes, transforming erotic pursuit into a kind of quest: 'Love is civilisation's miracle,' he writes, 'among barbarians and savages only physical love of the coarsest kind exists. And modesty protects love by imagination, and so gives it the chance to survive.' There is a degree of potential contradiction in this vision. Stendhal spends a number of chapters arguing for better education and greater freedom for women, arguing that sexual relations would be greatly improved as a result (it was this kind of thing that led Simone de Beauvoir to consider him one of the first feminists in her celebrated treatise *The Second Sex*). Nevertheless, he does also remain adamant that female pride and modesty, qualities that he freely admits to be closely linked to the continuing social inequality between the sexes, are absolutely necessary to the continuation of romance.

Stendhal was a liberal, and a supporter of greater freedom and equality; nevertheless, he was convinced that the march of nineteenth-century democracy would destroy the art of love. However much he might favour freer institutions in political terms, culturally he feared that such freedoms would interfere with human happiness by removing the adverse conditions in which love thrived. Perversely, it seemed to him, taking a survey of contemporary Europe, that those societies which were full of obstacles and inequalities – such as Bourbon Spain, or pre-unification Germany, or Italy under Austrian rule – were actually much more conducive to happiness than freer ones such as Britain or France, because of the way in which social barriers served both to provoke and sustain desire. 'A free government is one which does its citizens no harm, giving them security and tranquillity,' he wrote, with the United States clearly in mind, 'but this is a far cry from happiness, which is something a man must make for himself.'

Of all peoples, Stendhal considered the Italians to be the best lovers. They had everything going for them: they were beautiful, they were passionate, and the political stagnation of their country in 1821 meant that there was nothing whatsoever to distract them from romance. They also read very little, so their feelings were still natural and spontaneous; they hadn't been made self-conscious and affected by devouring too many novels. More to the point, there was no such thing as *ridicule* in Italy; there was no shame, no necessary loss of self-esteem, in becoming a fool for love. After the Italians came the Germans, inferior to their neighbours not through any lack of passion, but through an excess of it. According to Stendhal, young Germans were, if anything, too enthusiastic in their courtships, only too willing to throw themselves overboard if their love hit the rocks.

The French, on the other hand, were too knowing to be good lovers. They had all read too many books, and were too fearful of ridicule. Of a Frenchman in a grand passion, Stendhal wrote, 'I seem to see a man throwing himself out of a window but trying nevertheless to land gracefully on the pavement below.' What is more, he said, the French did not spend nearly enough time alone. Long periods of solitude were immensely important to the growth of love, Stendhal reasoned, for it was only through boredom and brooding that its seedbed would be prepared. Not only were the French too sociable, they also took too much pride in their own sophistication. Hence love in France was almost always mannered love or vanity-love, as in Laclos' *Dangerous Liaisons*, where the male and female characters were always far too conscious of playing a part.

That said, the French were still a good deal better than the English, whom Stendhal considered to be the saddest nation alive. English women were far too virtuous to make good lovers, he said, and the men were far too proud: 'No man here wants to press forward,' he wrote, 'in case he should be disappointed in the attempt.' That's why the women spent all their evenings knitting and sewing together, while the men just went off to get gloomily drunk. Last of all came the Americans, whose practical, commercial spirit had rendered them completely immune to romance: 'There is such a *habit of reason* in the United States,' Stendhal said, 'that the crystallisation of love there has become impossible.'

For Stendhal, the high point in the history of romance was during the twelfth and thirteenth centuries, when the aristocratic courts of Provence were governed by an elaborate code of love. This code, Stendhal tells us, imposed strict regulations on the manner in which a lover should declare his devotion to his lady, and the way in which his preferment should proceed. Husbands were left completely out of the picture, largely because most marriages were arranged, nevertheless a lady's official promotion of lovers was not supposed to go beyond the bounds of the most tender friendship or affectionate patronage. Some degree of personal preference must have been inevitable, of course, but the idea was that a lover graduated from stage to stage, from one formal intimacy to another, by pure merit alone. According to this system, a woman might have several lovers, but only one among the higher grades. With her favoured knight, something approaching a private relationship might develop, but such connections were only tolerated in the very public world of the medieval castle as long as they were pursued with discretion. The lady would communicate with her lover by means of signs, secret gestures, glances, and the wearing of particular emblems, and it was the lover's privilege to be the master of this code. The same privileges would not have been extended to her other lovers, however: they would not have been promoted much beyond the degree of friendship that allowed them to see their lady every day and kiss her hand.

Ostensibly, Stendhal admits, so much publicity and formality might seem at odds with genuine passion, but in fact the culture of courtly love was suffused with extraordinary delicacy and deep feeling.

If a lady said to her courtier:'For my love's sake, go and visit the Sepulchre of Our Lord Jesus Christ in Jerusalem. Stay there for three years and then return to me,' the lover would depart instantly. A moment's hesitation would be as ignominious as weakness in an affair of honour in our own day.

Stendhal was surely right to go back to the troubadours.

This historical moment, strange as it was, did represent an important step on the road to civilisation, for it was a noble advance upon the warrior culture that had preceded it. With this change, the role of women was transformed. They were no longer mere status symbols, purely passive emblems of their husband's virtue. They became guardians and judges of virtue in their own right; and virtue itself became softer and more civilised in their hands; that is, more about goodness than strength. It was, as many writers later recognised, the first feminist moment, but it was also a moment in which the dividing line between requited and unrequited love was usefully blurred. Love, under this dispensation, was subject to innumerable checks and trials, but possession – consummation – was not the final goal. The presumption was that romantic love should be encouraged because it was, in itself, an improving passion, a proof of the immortality of the soul. With us in the twenty-first century, distant passion has a pale and misguided air, but the troubadours wore their fraying hearts like badges of distinction. There was no shame in them devoting their lives to their mistresses and receiving only orders and injunctions in return, because it was understood that the passion between a lover and his beloved was a noble commitment, a dedication to a higher cause.

It was under the influence of courtly love that Europe

developed the concept – as well as the practice – of romance. In the late medieval period, romance was a literary genre, a narrative in prose or verse dealing with heroic deeds and chivalry. But the word has sprouted countless additional meanings since then. Now it refers to anything romantic, fantastical, formulaic or sentimental, anything at one remove from 'real' life. In essence, however, romance is much more than just a form or a formula. It is love conceived in terms of a quest. Romance is whatever obstructs (and thereby helps to define) desire. Prospero is invested with the spirit of romance when he uses his magic to slow down the courtship of Ferdinand and his daughter Miranda in *The Tempest*: 'Lest too light winning make the prize seem light.' So too, romance is the balcony that separates Romeo from Juliet, prompting him to look up and say: 'See how she leans her cheek upon her hand./O that I were a Glove upon that hand,/That I might touch that cheek.' But romance is also Juliet, in the same scene, refusing to be rushed:

It is too rash, too unadvised, too sudden,
Too like the lightning which doth cease to be
Ere one can say it lightens. Sweet, good night:
This bud of Love by Summer's ripening breath,
May prove a beauteous flower when next we meet.

Romance is a pilgrimage, a trek, a great sea voyage. It is a thorny hack through the dense forest to the princess's castle. It is a search for love – but it is a search in which the experience of seeking changes the nature of what is sought. Romance is the education of desire.

Even in the most unrequited of love affairs, there are lessons to be learned. Looking for a single slip or sign in the face of our beloved, trying to rearrange the details of his or her behaviour into a little conspiracy of love, we are reminded of the significance of small things, of the hidden meaning behind appearances. Love makes us see the world anew, or reminds us of what we had almost forgotten. To Stendhal it was, first and foremost, a solitary condition, a state of extreme subjectivity; a game that you played on your own. 'Love', he said, 'is the only passion that rewards itself in a coin of its own manufacture': in other words, it is a form of internal alchemy long before it becomes a medium of exchange.

Stendhal was a fetishist at heart, hence the perverse pleasure he took in all the endless distractions of romance. To him, it was quite possible to be happy and fulfilled in love regardless of whether one's passion was fully returned or consummated. Indeed he regularly flirted with the idea that lovers might be happier not getting what they want. Certainly, when reading *On Love* the suspicion does arise, from time to time, that he himself was never more exhilarated than when engaged in a distant devotion to a chilly contessa, to be fed perhaps once every two weeks by an hour of super-charged *conversazione*.

To some extent, however, such chaste tastes had been forced upon him. In the summer of 1819, at the height of his one-way passion for Mathilde, Stendhal decided to pursue her all the way from Milan to the little hilltop town of Volterra, where she had gone to visit her two sons. He was desperate to be with her, but feared that she might not take kindly to his presence, so he changed his clothing and put on some thick green spectacles, planning to follow her around *incognito*. It was one of the least effective disguises in romantic history. No sooner had he got off the coach at Volterra than Mathilde had both seen and identified him; somehow or other, his amorous camouflage had failed to fool her, and she was livid with rage. Heartily indignant that he had tried to follow her, she threatened to withdraw her friendship forever. Stendhal, for his part, felt very wounded by her seeming cruelty, and tried – quite unsuccessfully – to get angry himself. In the end, however, he backed down, and from that moment on his love for Mathilde was fuelled solely by correspondence and polite conversation, and he never tried the same trick again. Goodness knows what Stendhal thought he was doing dressing up in that fashion. Perhaps the spectacles were only ever a kind of clumsy metaphor, a means of betraying himself through his disguise. For not only did they show his eyes to be green – green with innocence, perhaps, or possibly jealousy. They were also ludicrously visible – a perfect emblem for the true lover as the most transparent of conspirators, the most conspicuous of voyeurs.

Stendhal had no desire to bring back the strict codes and antiquated hierarchies of medieval society, but he was worried that modern manners – the openness and practicality of the modern age – would destroy the art of love. From a rational point of view, he could see that romance was not very productive. It didn't make careers, or babies. Nevertheless, he wanted to show that, from another perspective, it was an essential part of the quest of life. That's why unrequited love had such an important place in his schema: it foregrounded love as an essentially imaginative experience, an experience that was all about the extension rather than the consummation of desire.

You hear a traveller speaking of the cool orange groves in the summer heat beside the sea at Genoa: Oh, if only you could share that coolness with her!

Distant passion, in this formulation, is not a juvenile distraction from the business of life, but its ideal companion. It turns the lover into a curator of little details, a seeker of connections, a connoisseur. It brings out the poet in us all. 'It is because he is emotionally nourished upon reverie and because he hates vulgarity,' Stendhal wrote, 'that a great artist is always so close to loving'. But was he right in thinking that modern society would have too few obstacles to keep such feelings alive, and that the citizens of a democratic age would be far too sensible to cultivate unrequited love? Or did he underestimate how far the insurmountable – and the irrational – would continue to characterise modern life?

IV

To us, unrequited love is unrequired love – impractical, unproductive and unreal. At best it is pathetic, at worst, pathological. Either way, we see it as a kind of category mistake, a failure of the reality principle. Outside the realm of poetry and song, its two safe havens, hopeless passion has come to seem, well, hopeless. It is a series of unanswered phone calls and misdirected texts. It is the story of something too insubstantial to turn into a story. It is an emotional dead-end. We take an increasingly hard-headed attitude to such misplaced investments. We tell our friends to 'get over them' as if they were merely little troughs in the great trek. As the poet John Suckling expressed it very nearly four hundred years ago:

> Quit, quit for Shame! This will not move,
> This cannot take her;
> If of herself she will not love,
> Nothing can make her:
> The Devil take her!

If anything, the shame attached to unrequited love has only increased since Suckling's time, which is odd, given that the experience itself is as universal as it ever was. Every passion, after all, is unrequited at the beginning, and for many the period of early youth is entirely made up of remote, ill-focused and invariably unfulfilled desires. There is something admirable as well as ridiculous about such crushes, for by fixing upon a distant object in our teenage years, what we are perhaps expressing, whether we are aware of it or not, is a longing for the future, for a time when our circumstances will be transformed out of all recognition, and our life will begin in earnest; and often the very remoteness of this object bears witness to an unconscious acknowledgement on our part that we are going to have to be patient with this longing, that fulfilment is going to have to wait. Not the object only, but also the obstacle, helps define the desire. But why is it so difficult to think well of such experiences when they occur in later life? Is it a natural feature of growing up that we should want to put away such childish things? Or is it something to do with modern culture that we can no longer think of unrequited love as an improving passion? Does stalking reveal the truth about unrequited love – its selfishness, its neediness, its fundamentally juvenile quality – or is it a sign of our degeneracy that we can no longer think of it except in these terms?

Sometimes I am tempted to think of the last two millennia as being like the first twenty years of an individual's life. First come the dark ages, which are like a kind of extended latency period, during which, as all the best-informed historians agree, most people spend their time howling and beating each other over the head with sticks. Then come the twelfth and thirteenth centuries – the early teens – when love blossoms for the first time. I imagine the entire courtly love period as a time when the cult of the crush is king, when love is innocent and tender, and when everything conspires both to encourage and yet also to regulate romance. With the early modern period – from the fifteenth to the nineteenth centuries – I see a more urgent and implacable spirit entering the conduct of love. The modern drive towards individual freedom begins to be felt. Poets and writers start to use frustrated desire as a means of criticising the social order, a means of railing against aristocratic prejudices and arranged marriages, the traditional restrictions of gender and class. Suddenly unhappy love becomes political – the complaint of the rebellious teenager – and takes on a heroic cast. Last of all come the twenties – our own particular age – when love is divested of all its former restrictions, and of half its charm.

Only love is unrequited. We are forced to speak of friendships as unreciprocated, and of favours going unreturned, because the word unrequited will accept no partner but love. How strangely apt that this quaint-sounding adjective, dating back to Shakespeare's time, should have survived into our own age by fixing itself, as it were obsessively, to one of the most celebrated and sought-after nouns. The very word is a kind of stalker. So much so, indeed, that one cannot say it without conjuring up the idea of love as its absent partner, the fair sun to its unhappy shadow. According to the *Oxford English Dictionary* to requite is, first and foremost, to repay, to make return for, to reward. But its source in medieval Latin does also suggest another layer of meaning, one that is still very much present in our own understanding of the term. For *requite* comes from the medieval Latin word *quitus* = unmolested, free, clear; and it is from *quitus* that we get the verb to quit = to leave, to cease, to discharge oneself (as from a burden or a debt). It is also the source of the adjective *quite* = completely, totally, as in 'Have you *quite* finished?' To be unrequited, then, is not quite the same as going unrewarded, for the condition it describes is one in which another person's unpaid debt to us actually results in our being left in a state of bondage. It is to be caught in a kind of spell, suspended, unredeemed. Its deep root is in the Latin word *quietus* = quiet or at rest, a word which makes an unexpected appearance in one of the most famous speeches in all English literature, the 'To be or not to be' soliloquy from *Hamlet*, when the prince ponders how easy it would be for a man to do away with himself with the single prick of a needle: 'When he himself might his quietus make with a bare bodkin.' By 'quietus', Hamlet means an action that brings about a complete release from life, a quitting that would also be a making quiet. Somewhere beneath the surface of the phrase 'unrequited love' there is a deep longing for this kind of quiet: it suggests a love of freedom so total and complete that death may be its only deliverance.

Significantly, it was in 1542, in Sir Thomas Wyatt's 'Complaint for True Love Unrequited' that the phrase first came into currency, as if to herald the birth of something modern. Wyatt's phrase brought a new depth to the discussion of unhappy passion, registering the utter alienation of those excluded from the charmed circle of courtly love; the ambition – and frustration – of the man or woman on the outside. At the beginning of Shakespeare's comedy, *Twelfth Night*, Illyria is full of unrequited lovers, but by the end of Act V, Viola and Orsino, Olivia and Sebastian, Sir Toby and Maria have all been paired off. The only man left wanting is the upstart servant Malvolio, who had been duped into believing that his mistress Olivia wanted to marry him and raise him up. 'Some are born great, some achieve greatness, and some have greatness thrust upon them,' he is told, in the fake letter from Olivia forged by Maria and Toby Belch. Much ridiculed and abused for his 'self-love' and ambition, for having dared to aspire beyond his station, Malvolio remains unreconcilable at the end of the play: 'I'll be revenged on the whole pack of you,' he says, before storming off the stage.

Unrequited Love is Unquiet Love. It is impatient with social obstacles, and dismissive of religious distractions. It refuses to be fobbed off. Its model of love is not based on bondage, but on a release from bondage. It is all about freedom, not service. Hence in the Renaissance period, the figure of the unrequited lover often carries with it a kind of submerged protest against class and gender restrictions. That is presumably why Malvolio, ridiculous as he is, never fails to prick our conscience at the end of *Twelfth Night*, and why we are always so sympathetic to Helena, the doctor's daughter from *All's Well That Ends Well*, who spends the entire play unrequitedly in love with the snobbish duke Bertram. For Malvolio and Helena are the true moderns at the heart of Shakespeare's comic court: in them, distant passion has a revolutionary aspect.

With the onset of the late teens, the literature of unrequited love becomes even more political in character. The frustrated lover is increasingly a figure of social protest. In one of the world's first tragic novels, Johann Wolfgang von Goethe's *Sorrows of Young Werther* (1774), the hero, who is a bright and enthusiastic young scholar from the German middle class, falls deeply in love with a woman called Charlotte. The problem is that Charlotte is already betrothed to another man, Albert, a very upright if slightly stuffy civil servant, whom she later marries. At first Werther is a dear friend to the couple, spending long evenings in their company, reading poetry, looking at engravings, and listening to Charlotte play the piano. But gradually he becomes increasingly withdrawn in Albert's company, and ever more melancholy in Charlotte's.

To many eighteenth-century English readers, Werther's love-lorn passivity was rather pathetic, and even Charlotte eventually grows tired of having to watch him sob all over the carpet: 'Be a man!' she says, 'Put an end to this dismal attachment to a creature who can do nothing but pity you.' But the French novelist and critic Germaine de Staël probably got it right when she said that Werther's predicament was not pathetic but tragic, because it was all about the condition of a sensitive soul under a bad social order. Midway through the novel Werther resigns his position at the local court, being too proud to accept the degree of class apartheid that is being demanded by the local aristocracy. But above and beyond the class obstacle Werther faces, there is a geographical one as well. Germany was still a disconnected patchwork of little principalities at this time. It was still not easy to move from one state to another. Werther is forced to kick his heels in the provinces because he has nowhere else to go; he is like a frustrated teenager who is unable to leave home.

'People tell of a noble breed of horses', he tells a friend in a letter, 'that instinctively bite open a vein when they are exhausted and feverish, in order to breathe more freely. I often feel the same, and am tempted to open a vein and so find eternal freedom.' And it is in this mood, with his professional hopes buried in the dust, that Werther's love for Charlotte grows into a self-destructive obsession, an obsession that finally results in him committing suicide by shooting himself in the head.

To the last, Werther's investment in Charlotte is double-edged, paradoxical. As Charlotte herself recognises: 'I very much fear that what makes the desire to possess me so attractive is its very impossibility.' He fixes upon her because she is a fine example of all that is best and most forward-looking about German bourgeois culture – she is sensitive and passionate and open. But he also wants her precisely because he can't have her; her unattainability is a perfect symbol, in this respect, of all the other obstacles that have got in his way.

The Romantic period saw a heroic assault on such obstacles. America revolted against British rule in the 1770s. The French Revolution, a concerted attack on aristocratic privilege, erupted in 1789. There were liberal insurrections in Spain and Greece, and slave revolts in the Caribbean. And at a less dramatic level, there was an eloquent campaign in the literature of the period against arranged marriages, and in defence of cross-class love. It was a progressive age, an age of 'improvement', in which developments in industry and commerce were breaking down geographical and social boundaries, and bringing a freer, more open Europe into being. In extraordinary poems such as *The Revolt of Islam*, which describes an imaginary revolution against despotic rule taking place in contemporary Turkey, Percy Bysshe Shelley depicted men and women as equals, soulmates, united in love and work. Even Jane Austen's novels, conservative though they are, contain a heartfelt critique of aristocratic exclusivity, and an eloquent defence of a woman's right to choose. Indeed, it is in this period that women first begin to write about desire for the first time. Women had written of love and romance before, of course, but most of the abandoned women of Western literature, figures such as Dido and Phèdre, and Helena from *All's Well That Ends Well*, had been ventriloquised by men. Now women were beginning to describe desire of the raw, unredeemed and unrequited kind. And as with Goethe, their motive was not merely personal but political. For in the eyes of revolutionary feminists such as Mary Wollstonecraft, de Staël, and Madame Roland, romantic desire was a means, not merely of asserting their own subjectivity, but also their right to be political subjects. It was a principled reproach to the French Revolutionaries of 1791, who had promised a constitution based on liberty and equality, only to finally produce one that denied women the vote.

Of all these radical women, Mary Wollstonecraft, the mother of Mary Shelley and the author of the *Vindication of the Rights of Woman*, was perhaps the most eloquent. Her *Letters from Sweden, Norway and Denmark* of 1796 is a powerful document of real-life romantic despair. She wrote the original letters during a business trip to Scandinavia, a trip that she had taken on behalf of her lover, the American adventurer and entrepreneur Gilbert Imlay, the man with whom she had been cohabiting in revolutionary France, and the father of her first child, Fanny. In the first series of letters Wollstonecraft struggles to combat an increasing sense of estrangement from her 'demon lover' Imlay, before finally deciding to transform her feeling of abandonment into a form of political protest.

Wollstonecraft suppresses the business element of her trip in the published version of her letters, choosing instead to represent her journey through the mountains of Sweden and Norway in highly romantic, not to say utopian terms – as the desperate search of an educated, sensitive and independent woman for a place where she might feel at home. And by suggesting that there is nowhere, at this point in history, that can successfully house such a creature, she turns her status as a female vagabond into an index of how much Western civilisation still has to achieve.

In her emancipated attitude to love and sex, Wollstonecraft looks beyond the late teens of Western culture to our own period, the early twenties, a time when many of the social and sexual obstacles that prevailed in the past have been surmounted and broken down. Very few of our loves are impossible now: cohabitation, divorce, adultery – these are all increasingly commonplace. Now more than ever, love is a simple matter of individual choice; no longer is it so easy to blame any lack of success on an unjust social order. Perhaps that is the reason why unrequited love is no longer the heroic subject it was in former times; and why it has become increasingly synonymous with failure.

Wollstonecraft looks forward to the old obstacles being swept away, but she also anticipates the emergence of a new one, blaming the breakdown of her relationship with Imlay on his increasing obsession with commerce. To many people commerce is a communicator, a facilitator, a means of mutual enrichment; but to Wollstonecraft it was a distracting fever, a kind of dust cloud of the understanding. It was a means of losing the spirit of freedom in the pursuit of free trade:

> Ah! shall I whisper to you – that you – yourself, are strangely altered, since you have entered deeply into commerce – more than you are aware of – never allowing yourself to reflect, and keeping your mind, or rather passions, in a continual state of agitation – Nature has given you talents, which lie dormant, or are wasted in ignoble pursuits – You will rouse yourself, and shake off the vile dust that obscures you, or my understanding, as well as my heart deceives me, egregiously – only tell me when?

V

One of my new friends in London was an American woman called Claire. She had a secret flow chart to assess prospective suitors. She had built it up painstakingly, over time. It helped her, she said, to remain objective about the men in her life, and to assess their potential. Mostly, the men in question would follow well-worn channels of behaviour; on rare occasions, however, one of them would scuttle off and start describing some crazy pattern of his own. This meant that if the relationship then proceeded to break down, the loss was by no means total. A new link could always be added to the map, and new knowledge gained. Hard-won as much of its wisdom was, Claire still considered the flow chart indispensable. It was building into a comprehensive guide.

'I can't show it to you, of course,' she said. 'But I can give you an idea of the kind of thing it has on it. For example, the chart tells me that I should never accept a date from a man who phones up on a Tuesday or a Wednesday.'

'*Right*. And why not?'

'Because in my experience such men are badly organised, desperate and insincere'.

'Badly organised, desperate *and* insincere?'

'Well – a better organised man would have phoned earlier in the week. A man who phones you on a Tuesday or a Wednesday has suddenly realised that the weekend is looming ahead of him like some arctic waste, and is using you as his shot of brandy. So you see, badly organised, desperate and insincere.'

'I do see,' I replied, feeling rather anxious, 'but isn't this a bit too much like *The Rules*?'

'No – because it's personal. It's a product of personal experience. *The Rules* is far too general.'

'But surely the problem is not so much that we don't learn from our past experiences, but that we always learn too much. We never want to be hurt in the same way again, and so we make wild generalisations – based on a single instance. I mean, if I were to think of my past in that way, I can't think what ridiculous conclusions I would be forced to draw – that I should never go out with scientists, doctors, nurses or lawyers. And that I should always be wary of girls who can draw on their legs without using a pen. But you can't do that to people – people are individuals. One shouldn't translate them into types in this way.'

'One shouldn't turn them into silly types. Your relationship with the last girl can't have broken down simply because she scribbled on her legs.'

'Well, no. It was a very attractive habit, actually. She had such sensitive skin that she could take a pencil and write "Hello Greg" on her upper thigh.'

'How wonderful,' said Claire, 'to be able to cover one's body with reminders of one's mistakes.'

'Oh – I think it wore off eventually', I mumbled, 'with time.'

My twenties had been taken up by two long relationships – until recently, I had never played the dating game. So it was a shock to strike thirty and enter the age of anxiety. Like me, most of the women I met were all in the fourth decade. They all had a history of having been deep with someone else, of having been involved. Now they were seeking a new involvement, while also being very wary about what that might entail. If the past was construed in terms of a series of mistakes, and frequently it was, they were determined not to repeat them. There were to be no more false starts. Sometimes it was children who haunted the courtship, drove it on; sometimes just a weariness of being alone. The problem was that, in one's thirties, commitment was being demanded right from the beginning. The time of courtship had shrunk almost to nothing. There was now no obstacle – but there was also no time. Fleeing from the pressure of this, my love life had become exactly like *The English Patient* without the war, the people or the planes: a vast desert.

The thirtysomethings I knew were extremely mindful of the peculiar privileges of our age; no previous generation had enjoyed so much freedom. But in some ways that only made our predicament more paradoxical. All of the frustrations of adolescence, its ungainly furniture, had been cleared away, no longer were there any parents or college cliques to get in the way. We had evacuated our youth. But taking stock, one realised that there was something equivocal about the wide, open space that we had entered into. No longer were we surrounded by vast crowds of young people hanging off one another's arms. The world's atmosphere had grown thinner, more rarified. Freedom's vanishing point was getting near.

In theory, cities are very promising places to find love: the Londoner tells herself that somewhere in the five zones there must be a person with whom she will be compatible. The problem is, of course, how does she go about locating him? And perhaps just as problematically, how will she know when she has? Come to think of it, why should she think solely in terms of 'the one' in any case, given the wide variety of men on offer? Could it be that the theoretical vastness of the choice presents her with a very real practical problem: why pick one man rather than another? One of the benefits of having a partner is that they protect you from the rest of the world. They defend you not merely from your relatives, but from relativity. But to live as a single person in the city is to live in a near-paralysing state of possibility: it is to feel that one has too many choices to make about too many things.

In past centuries, one's choice of partner was probably quite limited; if one was a woman, one may not have had any choice at all. Now, however, the assumption of our modern media culture is that all the old obstacles have been dismantled, and that there is nothing to stop one looking beyond one's race, age or class. The field of selection is huge. Hence many metropolitans approach the singles scene like canny consumers, maintaining a degree of reserve, keeping their options open, always half-convinced that there will be someone more attractive, or more suitable, at the next table, or in the next bar. Try as they might, they are too sophisticated to get swept up by love's sweet madness; and find themselves remaining deeply pragmatic – and oddly calculating – throughout. In his essay 'On the Metropolis and Mental Life', the German sociologist Georg Simmel showed how city dwellers develop extreme forms of rationality in an attempt to process the continuing chaos of the city, but what Simmel didn't acknowledge, is that they often feel the need to react violently against this over-intellectualising tendency too. Perhaps this is the reason why even the most blasé and world-weary metropolitans still tend to harbour a secret belief in romantic destiny – in Mr. (or Ms.) Right – as if deep down they are still crying out for fate to save them from shopping.

In Dante's time, social transactions were still dominated by gift and barter. But from the Renaissance onwards money began to establish itself, ever more exclusively, as the universal intermediary. All but invisible in itself, money nevertheless transforms the way we see things. It makes us think of them as commodities, that is, as things capable of being exchanged. Football players, cancer drugs, chocolate bars, paintings: it doesn't matter how different things are, the commodity system makes us feel that they are all commensurate with one another. In a world in which everything has its price, all things can be weighed on the same scale. Forced into fierce competition with one another, commodities must adapt and change in order to survive. They are like species in Darwin's system of natural selection: constantly transforming themselves in order to keep their 'brand' alive.

Initially at least, this system is extremely exciting, both liberating and diversifying consumer desire. The problem is that, in time, the money economy does also tend to flatten one's sense of the particularity of things. As Simmel expresses it: 'Money, with all of its colourlessness and indifference, becomes the common denominator of all values; irreparably it hollows out the core of things, their individuality, their specific value, and their incomparability. All things float with equal specific gravity in the constantly moving stream of money.' This is one of the main reasons, Simmel argues, why city dwellers take such a bored and superior attitude to the world they live in, why they are so rational and reserved: 'The large cities, the main seats of the money exchange, bring the purchasability of things to the fore much more impressively than do smaller localities. That is why cities are the genuine locale of the blasé attitude.'

With increasing fervour, we look to love as a kind of antidote to this situation. We want it to break through reserve, restore a sense of individuality, and reaffirm the idea of incomparability and specific value. The problem is that, whether out of defensiveness or through force of habit, all too often we pursue love nowadays in exactly the same spirit as we pursue commodities – that is, as consumers. Ever more likely to have been involved in more than one relationship by the time we reach our late twenties, we start to compare and contrast partners, weighing up their good and bad qualities as if they were competing brands. Nowadays, if we want to register somebody's attractiveness to a third party, we will habitually compare them to this or that film star, representing them as if they were cheaper versions of something else. Sometimes this logic of substitution works to assuage amorous frustration; it is always there to cheer us up after a break-up by insisting that there are 'plenty more fish in the sea'. But it is not good at telling us why we can't have the particular fish we choose. Especially as the psychology of money has been telling us all along that it is desire, not virtue, that will get us what we would like – as if it is all a question of how badly we want something, not how much we deserve it. The commodity system tells us that if something is available, then it is there to be had. Increasingly, we are all possessed by this dream of possession. Perhaps that is why requited lovers are so fickle nowadays; and why unrequited lovers are so angry.

To ride the escalator on the underground is to engage in a little comedy of urban desire. In the 1830s the early Victorians thought it very amusing to ride on the omnibus, to sit facing one's fellow passengers while travelling sideways. How much funnier would they have found escalators? When you move onto the steps, you see an endless stream of people coming towards you on the opposing stairway, ascending slowly but inexorably out of the dark. The absolute regularity of this is such that there is something overly emphatic, something preposterously fateful, about their approach. Then, just as they get close, just as an approach is about to crystallise into an encounter, the line of people moves past us, like a train suddenly switching to another line. And as with a train, the effect is a kind of momentary incongruity, a comedy of flouted expectations. No matter how used we are to travelling on an escalator, buried deep within us is a continuing sense of surprise at this parting of the ways. The path of these lives runs close, but does not touch yours. They move forwards into your past. One feels foolish ever to have thought that it could have been otherwise. In this way escalators are designed to make us intrigued and curious about a series of people that we are never destined to meet. We are lifted up, carried, and then, at the end of every escalator journey, set back on our feet with a wry little shove. We feel a sudden discrepancy, an incongruity. The entire experience has the form of a joke.

Or, if the opposing escalator is further away, then other people figure differently again. They appear before us like a series of disconnected thoughts, or like the ads on the wall behind. To see a beautiful face, in such a context, is precisely to fall in love with an advertisement – to experience the other as a commodity, like a hat in a shop window, or a dish of conveyor-belt sushi. It is bizarre to be courted by one's food – for it to tootle round in little dishes, hoping to attract us as it goes by. So too it is a strange experience to be approached by people who are always moving away. In this context, unrequited love begins to take on a distinctly utopian quality: it has the heart of a country bumpkin crying out against the cruel choreography of the city. It has all the stupidity of trying to convert urban proximity into direct contact. In most city dwellers, the never-ending drama of love-at-last-sight eventually takes on the status of a cliché – it happens so often as to become banal. It is only those who are new to London who are likely to be struck by it – newcomers, and stalkers.

In 1840 the American writer Edgar Allan Poe published a story, set in London, which was entitled 'The Man of the Crowd'. The story begins with a German epigraph: *er lasst sich nicht lesen* – it does not permit itself to be read. The story is narrated by a man who is convalescing from a bout of sickness, and is looking out of the large bow-window of a London coffeehouse 'in one of those happy moods which are precisely the converse of *ennui* – moods of the keenest appetency, when the film from the mental vision departs...'

Relishing his return to life, the narrator takes an artist's delight in everything he sees, and he spends the first half of the story categorising the various members of the urban crowd, identifying businessmen, noblemen, gamblers and pickpockets, and making fine distinctions between the various types of clerk. To the experienced eye, he tells us, it is simplicity itself to deduce a man's profession and even his character from his general demeanour and manner of dressing – it is the easiest thing in the world for the experienced city dweller to put his fellow citizens in their place. As night descends, however, the narrator fixes upon one man, an old man, some sixty or seventy years of age, who had 'a countenance which at once arrested and absorbed my whole attention, on account of the absolute idiosyncracy of its expression'.

'How wild a history,' I said to myself, 'is written in that bosom.' Then came a craving to keep the man in view – to know more of him.

Stepping out of the café, the narrator starts stalking this creature, desperate to find out who he is and what he does. He trails him all night, along busy thoroughfares and down narrow, lonely streets, following him into gin-shops and bazaars. But he is unable to get any firmer idea about him, for the old man enters shop after shop, buys nothing, speaks no word, and looks at all objects with a wild and vacant stare. At last, the narrator relinquishes his pursuit, and turns aside to the reader in order to offer these final words:

'This old man', I said at length, 'is the type and genius of deep crime. He refuses to be alone. *He is the man of the crowd*. It will be in vain to follow; for I shall learn no more about him, nor of his deeds… and perhaps it is one of the great mercies of God that *er lasst sich nicht lesen*.'

It is a curious story – a tale in which nothing happens – a thriller without a plot. At the most obvious level, it reminds us of all those nineteenth-century anxieties about the growth of crime in the modern metropolis. But there is more to it than that. For in truth the story functions exactly like a dream, in which two quite contradictory wishes are being expressed at the same time. Overwhelmed by the bewildering variety of the city, Poe wants to be able to categorise and classify his fellow men; but he also wants them to be able to escape classification – to remain stubbornly and mysteriously themselves. Or, to put it another way, 'The Man of the Crowd' is haunted by two equal and opposite fears: one is that you can't trace the individual in the city – in which case the place will become an extremely terrifying and unpredictable place, a haven of crime. The other is that you *can*, in which case individuality itself starts to look like an endangered species, always about to be translated into a pre-existing type. By writing the story in this form, Poe tries to have it both ways. He tries to reassure us – and himself – that our fellow citizens are knowable, and that one can seek out the individual in the mass. But he also lets the principle of idiosyncrasy make its final getaway, keeping alive the notion that there is in all of us some ungraspable element that can never be pinned down.

This explains the narrator's need to let the old man go. Yet it also sheds light on his decision to follow him in the first place – for in choosing to follow this particular man for no obvious motive or reason, the narrator is effectively asserting his own absolute idiosyncrasy, his own difference from everyone else. Indeed, it is one of the most modern things about this story that it sees individuality – that which differentiates the individual from the crowd – as an essentially fugitive quality, something perverse and aberrant, an elusive spirit that is forever slipping through the net. Before the nineteenth century, one could argue, people had not worried about whether or not they were individuals; it is only in the age of statistics and standardisation that this anxiety begins to be felt. Perhaps the modern concept of individuality – of the individual as unique – is itself only a bi-product of the statistical age; a desperate attempt to defend ourselves from being categorised out of existence.

This is what distinguishes stalking from older forms of unrequited love: its roots in mass culture, in the experience of the urban crowd. For the crowd is not a community – it does not provide a web of personal relationships, a network of family ties. It is, on the contrary, a huge, abstract entity, immediate and yet remote, ever-changing and yet always the same. Hence modern city dwellers frequently find themselves developing a certain fantasy of particularity – of individual uniqueness – as a kind of antidote to the mass. Stalking, from one perspective, is nothing but an extreme version of this fantasy, the desire to affirm, as it were simultaneously, not merely the absolute particularity of the object (the person I am seeking is like no-one else), but also the absolute particularity of the subject (…and my love for her is utterly unique). Stalkers are people who have grown impatient with the game of metropolitan flirtation – or perhaps they were never allowed to play. They want to throw off reserve, and recover the old intimacy, short-circuiting the endless round of circulation and exchange. The problem is that, in the very intensity with which stalkers identify with identity, they end up destroying the thing they love. It is one thing to respect identity, to uphold it; it is quite another to want to identify with it, to seek a merger. Stalking is, in the truest sense, self-destructive, because it has an unconscious animus towards the object of its pursuit. Like Poe's narrator, stalkers always tend to think of their beloved's idiosyncrasy as not merely captivating but criminal – and criminal essentially because of its refusal to be caught.

VI

One consequence of my move to the city was that I started going to a gym. It was situated under the arches of a disused Victorian railway bridge on Wheler Street, the street next to mine. I had never attended a gym before, but this place was so convenient for me, and my need for exercise was so great, that I started to go quite regularly, in the evenings and at weekends. The gym was full of city people, employees of the nearby merchant banks, and artists and designers from Shoreditch and Hoxton Square. At least that's what I assumed they were – I never really got to know any of my fellow members as individuals, and so their actual identities remained opaque. Nobody talks in gyms. They are interstitial spaces, between work and home, where people go to be released from the pressures of sociability, and give their minds a rest. So much so, indeed, that if Jean-Jacques Rousseau were to come back to life and take a peek in a London gym, he might be forgiven for thinking that he had finally returned to his beloved state of nature. People wander semi-naked and free among a primeval forest of exercise machines. They look each other up and down, they may even engage in a little cold flirtation, but they never need to really relate or talk to one another. Even in shops, people converse. But the gym is a very post-modern achievement: a completely civilised, and yet utterly asocial space. There is something about its total lack of barriers, and the complete equality shared by all of its members, that renders it thoroughly inimical to conversation, indeed to intimacy of any kind, as if people are only too aware, while they are wandering about in their sports gear, of the need to maintain a kind of psychic distance from their fellow members, and keep themselves to themselves.

On first entrance, my gym appeared like a kind of underground workshop. The main room was a large, brightly lit chamber, packed full of exercise machines. The rowing and lifting machines were arranged in a long line parallel to the back wall, and faced by an unbroken series of full-length mirrors, which reflected back the entire room. The running and walking machines were arranged in rows on the opposite side of the room, all pointing towards a mounted triptych of TV monitors, which poured forth a seamless gospel of sport, glamour and MTV. Pop stars beamed down from above, beckoning us towards a distant land of health and beauty, while we pounded away doggedly on the rubber treadmills below. There was a purgatorial feel about the place. The machines, it seemed, were there to encourage us to climb towards immortality, the mirrors so we could see ourselves going nowhere in the attempt. There were no shadows anywhere. It was all very exposed.

Welcome distraction was provided by some of my fellow members, for whom I conceived a kind of familiar affection, albeit of the most distant kind. The men who did nothing but pump iron, pace up and down, and scowl at their reflections never failed to engage me, and I enjoyed watching the people who went into trances on the snow-shoe machine, like mountaineers climbing up an imaginary Everest. But most of all I liked the women who sat on mats, enclosed in a forbidden city of concentration, doing yoga or pilates. They made everybody else's exercises look strangely childish. Inevitably there were particular individuals whom I couldn't help wondering about, such as the man who blow-dried his chest in front of the main mirror in the gents' changing room. What precise pattern was he looking for –

or trying to avoid? But my relation to them all was purely spectatorial; I didn't talk to any of them, ever. Until, that is, about a year into my membership, when I spoke to the only girl I had ever been interested in. Or rather, she spoke to me.

She had brown eyes and short blonde hair, a clear, open face and a beautiful, broad smile. I had first become aware of her a few weeks before, towards the end of November, when she had smiled very briefly and casually as we swapped machines. It was a minor occurrence, a tiny lapse in gym etiquette. She had entered my mind like a slight breeze on an autumn day, a gentle threat, a threat so lovely and gentle that it left everything more or less as it had been, only a little more flushed and hectic than before. I don't know why it is that, often, the first feeling we are aware of entertaining towards the person we love is one of mild vexation. Perhaps it is envy, perhaps dismay, or perhaps it is simply a case of the body trying to steel itself against the inevitable suffering to come. No sooner has a breach been made in our hearts than repression rushes in to repair the damage, and our self-defence mechanisms are hard at work constructing their intricate, futile fortifications before we have any idea what they are actually defending us against. But such walls are seldom effective; being riddled with the very crevices to which crystallisation clings. Needless to say, the next time I saw her, a few weeks later, her extraordinary beauty broke upon me like a painful truth. I was hurt by it, damaged by it; it ran me through with a kind of careless, gratuitous violence. And when she smiled and spoke to me at first I couldn't hear a thing she was saying, there was such a dreadful wrenching and groaning in my head, as of a huge vessel being turned around.

Why had I fallen for her? There had been no calculation, no assessment. How wonderful not to have made a choice! Yet what was it that had drawn me to her, and not anybody else? Beauty, according to Stendhal, is only the promise of happiness. That is why we all have such different notions of where beauty resides. As Carson McCullers puts it in *The Ballad of the Sad Café*: 'A most mediocre person can be the object of a love which is wild, extravagant, and beautiful as the poison lilies of the swamp.' But what kind of happiness did her beauty promise me? And how had this promise been made? Of all the blondes in London, why her? Was it something in her tender brown eyes, or in that lovely open face? That smile, perhaps – so broad and generous: it said nothing, meant nothing, other than that life was incomparable, joyous. Was this smile a template for the future – or a reminiscence of the past? Did her face remind me, in some way, of some half-forgotten form that had guided me in my first childhood, of my mother when she was young, or one of my aunts? Or some other proud beauty, now long forgotten, whom I had told myself I could never aspire to? It was not possible to say.

Generally I tried to remain sceptical about such sudden conversions. None of my past relationships had started in this fashion. They had begun slowly and then grown richer and deeper with time. In my experience bolts from the blue were always precisely that – stray bolts of lightning, one-off events. They occupied a different realm from that of real experience – a country of paths not taken, of alternative lives. Perhaps it was right that they never went any further. Perhaps in a single epiphany they had already found their perfect form. At least that was the way I tried to think about them: not as missed opportunities, but as revelations of the mystery of life.

Reflecting on them retrospectively, it was quite possible to be calm and philosophical; but it was never so easy at the time. With this girl, I had no idea why I had fallen for her so suddenly and so heavily; it felt ridiculous, immature. But I couldn't stop myself. Before I knew it, I found all my saved-up wishes coming out. Never had it seemed less stupid or superficial to fall in love at first sight.

'You're here quite often aren't you?' she said, 'You must work out a lot.'

'I am shrinking,' I said, while also wondering whom it

was that was speaking these words, for they hadn't been what I had meant to say at all. 'I ought to stop.'

'Well – but you seem to be able to run for hours. I am such a lightweight.'

'I suppose I do come here relatively often. I live just around the corner, on Calvin Street, and it's a nice break from work.'

'I live on Brick Lane,' she volunteered. 'I used to have a flat near Victoria Park. But I moved here quite recently. It's great, isn't it?'

I nodded, and then she smiled at me again. 'You must be very fit,' she said.

'I'm very old,' I said, irrelevantly. And yet I did feel very old all of a sudden. It had been such a long time since I was last in love.

'You can't be that old,' she said, humouring me. 'But I know how you feel. I am twenty-six already.'

Twenty-six! It could have been worse, I suppose. She could have been twenty-two. Or eighteen. Thank heavens she wasn't eighteen.

'My name is Gregory,' I said, giving my Christian name in full, for some reason, and offering her my hand.

'Well, it's very nice to meet you, Gregory.' She spoke slowly, with a kind of deliberate kindness, as if to a small child. 'I'm Charlotte.'

'Charlotte, do you know that of all the people in the gym you are the one I most wanted to meet,' I said. 'I have never spoken to anybody else.'

Somehow this didn't come out quite right either. I had intended it as an indication that I didn't make a habit of chatting up girls on exercise machines, but it sounded a little too much like the opening words of The Creature when he meets his first human being.

'How funny,' she said. 'Why?'

' – I was just intrigued by you. You have such an interesting face.'

'Well I don't feel very interesting today. I have a hangover, and am wearing paint-splattered shorts.' She was very easy and carefree in her manner; her charm was perfectly natural. We were thousands of miles apart, she and I – she was clearly not in love.

'I don't find it very easy to talk here,' I said suddenly. 'It's such a terribly unsociable place. You wouldn't like to go out for a drink sometime, would you?'

This was a very glaring thing to say, but I knew how infrequent and erratic her gym visits were, and had become suddenly very afraid that, unless I arranged a meeting now, it might be a very long time before I saw her again.

'Maybe,' she said. 'I am seeing someone at the moment. But I don't see why not.'

'Well, you can think about it. Don't worry if it's not possible.'

Suddenly, out of nowhere, I felt a powerful urge to retract my offer, indeed to withdraw myself completely from her. It was the only gift in my power, I realised: the ability to relieve her, before she had even become aware of it, of the clumsy pressure of my infatuation.

We talked a little further, about our work, and about living in the East End. And then she said: 'Well, it was very nice to meet you, Gregory, but now you must excuse me. It's time for my swim.'

Twenty minutes later I wandered out to the pool myself. She came to the end of her length, and rose out of the water. Her smile was more radiant than ever.

'We have no means of getting in touch.' I said, 'Should I give you my phone number?'

'Let me give you my e-mail address,' she said, and spelled it out for me. 'I work for a media company. Based in Holborn. You can write to me there.'

Once out in the light, I could think of nothing else. I wrote to her immediately, saying how nice it had been to meet her, and suggested a time when we might go out for a drink. There was something terrifyingly transparent in my eagerness. It would not be necessary for her to read the letter in order to discover the urgency of my feelings, the timing would say it all. I knew it would have been better to have waited a few days, played it cool. But such tactics were beyond my power. With my foundations shaken, every hour brought some new subsidence of feeling. Sometimes it felt as if whole storeys were collapsing, caving in on one another, leaving huge hollow needs that I had never been aware of before. When she didn't reply the following day, I felt bereft. Of course, the absurdity of the situation was not lost on me: we were perfect strangers who had only exchanged a few sentences, and my sentences had been of the most idiotic kind. What kind of a basis for a relationship was that? Certainly, to build up one's hopes – to crystallise on so slender a basis – was pure madness. Nevertheless, there was already a string of little diamonds glittering on the bough.

A friend of Stendhal's once told him: 'When you're in love with a woman, you must ask yourself: what do you want to do with her?' The answer is never as obvious as one might think. In Charlotte's case, I imagined us walking the streets of the city together, visiting places, looking at things. 'Here', I would say, 'this is what I have discovered. This is for you.' In her company, all of the things I liked best – the buildings, the paintings, the music, the books – would have started to creep out of their hiding places, and the fallen and fading world would have been gradually but triumphantly redeemed. One didn't quite know how one had allowed these things to fall into neglect in the first place, but felt instinctively that they were still out there, in all their richness and variety, just waiting to be rediscovered. Without actually having been aware of doing so, I had deprived myself of these pleasures for quite some time, or, more properly, deferred them; as if I had felt that I needed some excuse, some justification, for staging the return to life, always waiting for some better reason to love the world.

Charlotte replied to my e-mail two days later. She said that she was not up on relationships between a man and a woman when one of them was already in a relationship, but she guessed that they were probably not a good idea. So she thought she ought to pass on the drink. But if we kept on bumping into one another in the gym and chatting, she thought that eventually it might be legitimate to meet up outside. It was a very good, sensible letter. I liked her use of the word 'legitimate'. Fine word, 'legitimate'. It made it seem as if she was doing what she was doing out of a respect for the rules, while secretly seeking to go beyond them, if only in the most innocent of ways. After speaking to her, my deepest wish had been that she had completely invented her boyfriend – as a kind of screen of the truth. Failing that, I had hopes that she was about to dump him. After all, 'I am seeing someone at the moment' hardly made him sound like the most permanent of fixtures. Her letter complicated but did not entirely explode this interpretation. It was quite possible that she was giving me the brush-off, but very indirectly and gently, so as not to hurt my feelings. But there was also a chance that she was trying to slow down the pace of our courtship, 'lest too light winning make the prize seem light'.

The problem for me, of course, was that I was clearly no good at gym conversation. There was something about the space and the atmosphere that I found impossible. But there was also a larger, more pressing issue: the fact that, where the gym was concerned, Charlotte hardly ever went. Perhaps she would exercise more often now, I thought. Even the most infinitesimal of changes in her behaviour might count as a sign. I knew that the best thing was simply to wait and see. In the meantime, however, I found my own devotion to the gym had increased alarmingly. Every evening I was rushing home from work and leaping straight onto the running machine. I hadn't seen Gabriel or any of my other friends for ages. With idiotic single-mindedness, I was turning down numerous invitations, dates and dinner parties in order to pound myself into the ground on a rubber road to nowhere.

A month later, I sat back and assessed the situation. Charlotte and I had exchanged another couple of e-mails. We had, it turned out, a number of things in common. We had both been to the same university as undergraduates, albeit at different times. She had also spent some time at my new institution, University College. In fact, for the whole of my first at year at UCL she would have been working in the building immediately opposite mine, studying for an MA in Archaeology and Anthropology. Now she wanted to move on, as I had done, to a PhD. I still knew very little about her, but what I had managed to discover had only deepened my investment, for it seemed as if we had been haunting one another's movements for quite some time.

But there was also a real communication problem as well. Not only had she neglected to reply to my fourth e-mail, we had also failed to bump into one another at the gym. There were a couple of conclusions to be drawn from this: firstly, that she was in no hurry to see me; secondly, that her boyfriend was almost certainly real, and not, as I had secretly been hoping, a woolly dolly like Anna. There were also a couple of unforeseen consequences to my increased gym-going. Exercising every day, and not eating properly, had started to do strange things to my body. I was growing more and more unfit, and the very few muscles I had managed to cultivate were, oddly enough, all on one side. One more month of this, I thought, and I will look like a hermit crab. And probably walk like one too. How would Charlotte feel about going out with a man who could only move sideways?

It didn't bear thinking about. Furthermore, such was the frequency of my visits that I was beginning to get funny looks from some of the women members. 'It's that creepy guy again,' I imagined them saying to themselves, 'why can't he walk forwards like everyone else?'

Still, it was worth it. One evening a couple of months later I had been pounding away on one of the running-machines, my eyes drifting across the high bank of TV monitors, when all of a sudden I became aware of a figure waving at me – or at somebody else – in the full-length mirror below. It was Charlotte, I think. She was waving and walking. She was waving at me and walking towards the door. She didn't know anybody else in the gym, so it was almost certainly me that she was waving to. But she was also walking briskly towards the door. I didn't wave back, because it was only after she had gone out of the door that I realised who it had been. What did it mean, this waving and walking? She had no need to wave – I had not spotted her until she started waving. And was the walking meant to qualify the waving, or was it the other way around? The more I thought about it, the more perplexed I became: what did it mean, what had she given me – a shy hello or a friendly goodbye?

Charlotte! Charlotte! When Goethe's Werther first met his Charlotte she had been in the entrance-hall of a little

German country house, handing out slices of bread to a group of little children, each according to their age and appetite. She was wearing a simple white dress with pink ribbons at the sleeves and breast. Only half an hour before, he had been warned by one of the local girls that he must take care not to fall in love with Charlotte because she was already promised to someone else, but the information had left Werther completely indifferent because she was, at that point, no more than a name. It was only much later that day, after accompanying her to a ball, and dancing with her, and being caught in a thunderstorm with her, and talking about German poetry with her, that he had been reminded of her betrothed condition, by which time it was already too late – he was head over heels.

Like Goethe's Charlotte, East End Charlotte was open, friendly, intelligent and sensible. And yet also like her literary ancestor, she was already taken. But perhaps there was just enough hope – or doubt – to warrant further pursuit. And yet what could I possibly hope to gain? The idea of forcing my way into her life, even successfully, was grotesque. The only positive scenario I ever had in my mind – which was scarcely a scenario at all – was one in which all our difficulties simply fell away, disappeared, and we could go off into the sunset together without a shot being fired. More often, however, I fell into imagining myself as a kind of Captain Dobbin to Charlotte's Amelia Sedley – spending long years in patient service while she pined for someone else.

There was a strong element of Thackeray in Captain Dobbin, I remembered, for the author himself was once in a similar position to the unsung hero of *Vanity Fair*, having been in love with a beautiful woman who was married to one of his friends. And like many novelists, Thackeray had striven to make up for the disappointments of life in art, by ensuring that, long and painful as Dobbin's period of suffering turns out to be, he does get to marry Amelia in the end. Why was it, I wondered, that so many novelists of the past had been so unwilling to leave their heroes unrequited? Had it been wish-fulfilment on their part, or a desire for poetic justice? Or was it because lovers who remain unrequited have a way of interfering with the balance of a story, making it seem somehow inadequate and incomplete? It is as if, by sticking like a fishbone in the throat of a plot, such lovers end up calling its very structure and scope into question, having a nasty habit of revenging themselves, not merely against their fellow characters, but against their author and readers as well. That is why unhappy lovers who survive to the end of a story can so often register a critique, not merely against the social and political conventions of their age, but against literary conventions as well. Regarded in this light, Malvolio can be seen as Shakespeare's way of criticising the rule that every comedy must end in multiple marriage. And *Eugene Onegin*, Alexander Pushkin's famous tale of two mutually unrequited lovers kept apart by emotional perversity and bad timing, is a playful satire on every reader's desperate desire for romance to become real.

Perhaps this also explains why poetry and pop songs are so comparatively comfortable with the expression of unrequited love – because they do not have to turn it into a story. The lyric mode, the mode of song, has always stood in a particular relation to the moment, and to the expressions of the moment, hence poetry often speaks of emotions that exist in a kind of everlasting present, that are intense but intransitive, powerful but unchanging. They speak of passions that last forever but do not need to go anywhere, of sufferings that do not have a story. Lyric provides a kind of safe haven for the expression of unrequited love for this very reason, because it doesn't matter how violent or angry the emotions in question happen to be, the form will always be there to contain them, to bind them up in its eternal moment, and save them from themselves. This is one of poetry's great achievements, that it can turn what is bitter into something beautiful, by shifting it from the literal into the metaphorical realm. Witness, for example, these lines from Yeats:

I became a man, a hater of the wind,
Knowing one, out of all things, alone, that his head
May not lie on the breast, nor his lips on the hair
Of the woman that he loves, until he dies.
O beast of the wilderness, bird of the air,
Must I endure your amorous cries?

I kept wanting to write to Charlotte – but I only had her e-mail address, and e-mail is the absolute antithesis of poetry and music, being a medium of literal demands. Looking back on the five e-mails I had sent her, I couldn't help wishing that they had been letters instead. Letters at least have a concrete, physical existence. They come in envelopes; they seem to understand the distinction between inner and outer, private and public. In their very form as well as in their mode of address, there is a kind of etiquette. E-mail, by contrast, is a very impatient and imme-diate medium. Bypassing the physical world, it comes out of nowhere, flashing directly upon the mind of its recipient as upon a blank screen. Or else it lies there in the inbox, dated and timed, like an explosive device slowly ticking itself down. No matter how hard we try to couch it in the appa-ratus of sociability, e-mail remains a profoundly asocial medium, at once intrusive and remote. I had taken great care over the admiring e-mails I had sent to Charlotte, for I was very concerned not to foist upon her any of the treatment Lucy had given me, but somehow or other the very medium itself had refracted and distorted what I had written, discovering a terrible urgency and importunity in everything I said.

Looking at them over again, I felt that my e-mails were always pressing for a more immediate intimacy than I myself had been seeking, or felt I deserved. They were like a series of thinly disguised ultimatums. By the third e-mail, even 'Dear Charlotte' had begun to take on a rather tense, threatening quality, as if spoken by an angry lover through gritted teeth. More than anything, it was the tonelessness of these messages that got to me. Even the rather courteous, light-hearted manner sounded false. The problem was that I had no other way of getting in touch with her. Between stranger and stalker, it seemed, there was no middle realm.

After Charlotte had failed to reply to my fifth e-mail, I decided that it would not be proper for me to pester her any longer, and so I returned to my books. I even wondered whether Stendhal, who was so good at analysing the psychology of love, might be able to explain my condition to me, and even suggest a cure. When it comes to falling in love, he told me, 'an absence of mistrust is not enough; there must be a weariness of mistrusting, and, as it were, courage must be impatient with the hazards of life.'

You are unconsciously bored by living without loving, and convinced in spite of yourself by the example of others… One day you come across someone not unlike your ideal; crystallisation recognises its theme by the disturbance it creates, and consecrates for ever to the master of your destiny what you have dreamt of for so long.

Perhaps this was the reason why I had fallen so suddenly and so deeply: I was on a kind of rebound from mistrust. In the background, there was my thirtysomething terror, and then, more recently, there had been that long, lean non-relationship with Lucy, in which the last stirrings of my self-confidence had been hunted to extinction. Perhaps that was why I had given myself so totally and completely to Charlotte, without knowing anything about her: I was tired of being cautious; I was bored with being suspicious; I was ready to live again. And what I liked about Stendhal's model was that, even as he pointed up the deep irrationality of my situation, he did also seem to acknowledge that the passion it generated might be completely genuine all the same; indeed that it might be all the more powerful for having been so long in preparation, like a slow-brewing storm.

Is love more powerful when we are old or when we are young? I know opinions are divided on the matter. I remember a friend of mine, a distinguished professor, who dismissed young love as nothing more than a kind of glandular experiment. It was only in the latter stages of life, he thought, that passion's meaning became clear. To him it was not first but last love that was the most painful – because in later life one invariably has so much more to lose. To fall in love in old age, he thought, was often to betray one's former life, one's reputation, one's family; it was to risk everything in a desperate attempt to affirm one's right to be alive. And yet precisely because late love is one of the last, best means of raging against the dying of the light, the disappointment, if and when it comes, is bound to be all the more devastating.

In chapter eight of *On Love*, Stendhal put down his own feelings on the matter. He cited a woman friend of his, who used to point out that young love must inevitably be the more powerful of the two, because it is so enthusiastic and pure, and utterly uncorrupted by adult scepticism. But he himself was of the opposite opinion, arguing that mistrust in later life can serve as a kind of enabling obstacle to romance. The older woman, he writes,

> ...crystallises only slowly; but whatever crystals survive her terrible ordeal, where the spirit is moving in the face of the most appalling danger, will be a thousand times more brilliant and durable than those of a sixteen-year-old, whose

privileges are simply happiness and joy. Thus the later love will be less gay, but more passionate.

I didn't know whether I was more passionate about Charlotte than I had been about the distant crushes of my youth, but I certainly felt that I had a good deal more at stake. Like every other thirtysomething, I was worried that I had actually lost the capacity to fall in love, and so when I had such a powerful reaction to Charlotte, a reaction that was so powerful as to be beyond all reason and calculation, it felt as if this could be my last chance. Needless to say, however, I recognised that it was no good trying to tell Charlotte this, because it would be impossible to say such a thing in an e-mail without seeming either crazy or insincere. So I retreated into passivity, increasingly mindful of what the middle-aged William Hazlitt had said in his *Liber Amoris* of the disastrous infatuation he had once conceived for his landlord's teenage daughter: 'This state of suspense is like hanging in the air by a single thread that exhausts all your strength to keep hold of it; and yet if that fails you, you have nothing in the world else left to trust to.'

Charlotte had told me that she lived on Brick Lane, which was just a couple of blocks east of where I was. It is a long, narrow street, connecting Shoreditch, Spitalfields and Whitechapel. I wondered which end she lived on. Snatching a glimpse of her leaving the gym, I had noticed that she turned right rather than left out of the main doors, making for the north exit of the railway arch; that is, for the Shoreditch side. Perhaps she lived on the section of the street just north of Bethnal Green Road. This district had been one of the most notorious sections of the East End in the latter half of the nineteenth century, a parish of 8,000 people possessing 17 public houses but not one church, and with a death rate four times higher than the rest of London. Nicknamed 'the Jago', it had a record of criminality second to none, and was regularly described in the Victorian newspapers as 'the sink of London'. But most of the old slums had passed away long ago. Now there was an extensive complex of early twentieth-century model dwellings in the area, a series of handsome redbrick tenements that fanned out in a large circle. In the centre was a place called Arnold Circus, which had a little raised garden, trees and a bandstand. The bandstand was in a rather dilapidated state, and the garden was neglected, but it was still an unexpectedly beautiful square, a sort of proletarian version of South Kensington. Perhaps it was at this end of the lane that Charlotte lived. Or perhaps she lived nearer me, closer to the old Truman & Hanbury Brewery, in among the bagel shops and Indian restaurants, the new galleries, boutiques and cafés. This part of Brick Lane was gloriously mixed, a blend of Bangladeshi and British youth culture, and an extremely lively place. As one of the centres of the Indian community in the East End, it was, in truth, a very safe and friendly area, but because so many of the narrow, dark Victorian streets still survived it did also continue to have a faintly gothic feel about it, only too believably the former haunt of Joseph Merrick the Elephant Man and, even more famously, Jack the Ripper.

Sometimes I would stroll down Brick Lane, gazing up at

the first and second floor windows, trying to catch a glimpse of Charlotte. What did she think of this neighbourhood? In one of her e-mails she had said that she had always wanted to live in the East End because that was where her mother had been brought up. With what feelings, I wondered, did she wander around these obsessive little streets, so closely argued and conspiratorial, so thick as thieves with history? On occasion, the prospect of bumping into her felt so imminent that I would be gripped by a kind of amorous terror. It was especially bad at night. Coming home from Liverpool Street after an evening in central London, I would stroll under the belt of bulb lights lining the brow of Spitalfields market, looking in at the windows of all the pubs and cafés dotted around its edge. But although I searched eagerly through the ever-changing sea of faces, I never found hers. And every time I came to the corner of the market, the thin white form of Christchurch, Spitalfields, would shuffle forth out of the darkness to greet me, like the sad ghost of Don Quixote.

At that time, the rhythms of London still held me in thrall. I would go to bed exhausted, my mind like a fraught junction, worn down by the nervous traffic of the day. Then I would be up again a few hours later, in time to hear the first trains rolling down into Liverpool Street station, and feel an immediate need to be up and about. Often I would fall out of bed and into the street, and make for the 24-hour bakery on Brick Lane, where queues of drowsy clubbers and off-duty cabbies would be waiting in line for fresh bagels and sweet tea. On one occasion, I took my bagel to Arnold Circus, and ate my breakfast on a bench. It was deep winter, and there were no leaves on the trees, but the little garden and bandstand still looked splendidly dappled in the early morning light. More usually, however, I kept on walking, doubling back west in the hope of catching Charlotte on her way to the office. I knew she worked in Holborn. That meant a quick walk through Spitalfields to catch the Central Line from Liverpool Street, or else a bus from nearby Bishopsgate, the 8 or the 242. So I would stroll in and out of the narrow streets on the off-chance of meeting her, looking through windows, doorways, and into half-secluded courts.

As the rush-hour approached, I would find myself drifting down Elder Street and Norton Folgate, old Huguenot streets lined with silk-weavers' mansions, and into Bishopsgate, the old entrance to the City, which was now shadowed on either side by big merchant banks. And from there it was but a short step to Liverpool Street station itself, vaulted and vast, a great cathedral of modernity, full of stairways and balconies, restaurants and shops. Sometimes I would arrive before the early morning hubbub had started, when the station was still tranquil and gleaming white. But one morning I was early enough to stumble upon the last phase of the cleaning process itself, catching a glimpse of the stray figures whose job it was to wash all the floors, stairs, and notice-boards, and bring the poor tired terminal back to life. However lacklustre and litter-strewn it was at the end of the day, it would always be hosed down and forced back into service by the morning, all ready to receive the first great wave of trains from Colchester, Cambridge and the eastern counties. I felt a sudden sympathy for Liverpool Street, and thought of Tennyson's Tithonus, a man cursed by immortality, begging his lover the dawn-goddess Aurora to take pity on him and let him die:

> Release me, and restore me to the ground;
> Thou seest all things, thou wilt see my grave;
> Thou wilt renew thy beauty morn by morn;
> I earth in earth forget these empty courts,
> And thee returning on thy silver wheels.

I walked out to one of the ticket barriers on the main platform. There I was at my station, looking out at all the tracks trailing off into the distance, but never making a single journey myself. Was this what my freedom had come to?

It occurred to me that in avoiding choices, commitments, in trying to remain forever in the realm of possibility, I too, in a way, had been trying to make myself immortal. More recently, I had even started to withdraw myself from my new friends and colleagues, from the infinite and various claims of others, seeking out a world in which there would be no such thing as loss or failure because there would never be anything to lose. Tithonus had wished for the same thing. But immortality, he had found, was not all it was cracked up to be. It meant growing older year by year, and yet never being able to die. It meant retreating to the edge of the world. For months, it seemed to me, I had been spending too much of my life in isolation, without coming up against any obstacle at all. Was I in danger of becoming, like Tithonus, a bridegroom wedded only to the morning? Was I turning into a ghost?

Everywhere I looked, over the empty concourse, and across the adjoining square, the whiteness was encroaching. Perhaps e-mail was my perfect medium after all – a colourless, toneless, deathless world, a world in which all one's messages were sent primarily to oneself. Walking back home past Spitalfields Market I noted that half of the old market had been fenced off for redevelopment, and so I went over to look at the plans. There was going to be a brand-new complex of shops and offices, and a large new public square.

Every year the City encroached a little bit further into E1. More offices and flats sprang up, more disused factories and shops were redeveloped. Creative and dynamic in many instances, this process was also blind and brutal in others. Delightful spaces were forever being destroyed. The architect's plan for the redevelopment of Spitalfields made it look as if the new piazza was going to be a vast, empty area – one of those ultra-modern public spaces that nobody knows how to use. It too was going to be white. Walking across it one would feel incongruous, exposed, a sitting duck for the security cameras fixed in their sniper positions high above.

White space is what you are left with when all obstacles are taken away. It is a collapsing of distance, of difference, a meeting of the same. I was weary of all these empty message boxes and big, blank spaces, of agarophobic modernity in all its forms. The endless twists and turns of the East End appealed to me more – they threw up a whole series of beautiful distractions; indeed they re-established beauty itself as a kind of distraction, a much-needed detour from the thundering thoroughfare of life. This is what I had come to associate Charlotte with – this is why I needed her. Somewhere in the little cat's-cradle of streets that made up this region, she was to be found. Little crystals of imagination had formed on pub signs, doors and windows. I saw her, and worshipped her, everywhere. Curiously enough, however, the more intensely I attended to my surroundings, the less lovelorn I felt. The ardour and frustration were still there – and yet slowly but surely these feelings began to be combined, and then superseded, by other things. Before long, the very thing that was getting in the way of Charlotte and me, the scruffy jumble of Brick Lane, had started to become an all-absorbing fetish in my mind. Little details were becoming noticeable to me again – as they had been when I had first arrived. The entire area was being resurrected under her influence. Something had interposed itself between us, but it wasn't e-mail or the gym. They were too blank and too cold to act as real obstacles. The true obstacle, the enabling obstacle, was Spitalfields itself.

Washed up by the white sea of abstraction, I immersed myself in particulars, sinking my fingers into the heavy shingle of the here and now. And under this new dispensation, desire itself began to change its character. No longer was it a straight avenue, a busy thoroughfare, a great journey to a distant end; it was more of a sideways movement, a sidelong view, something that pulled and snagged. Increasingly, it was not where the arrow pointed that interested me, but how it was painted; not what the advertisement sold, but what it said. I was less and less interested in the city as a dream factory, billowing deep into the night, than as a concrete entity, in which human aspirations had found material form. For in so many of these streets, cramped and crumbling as they were, there was a powerful idea, a commitment even, to the idea of social space. Little courts and corners, disused gardens, rows of shops; they all provided a series of unfulfilled inklings, trapped hints, of how urban community might work. Slowly but surely, I returned to the enthusiasm of my first summer. But this time people were at the heart of it. As the memories of my relationship with Lucy receded, the claims of others no longer seemed quite so oppressive; now they started to appear as a strengthening as well as a binding force, a network tethering one to a particular place and time. Tentatively, and a little sheepishly, I started making efforts to pick up my old friendships.

In pacing around the East End as one would walk around a stage set, waiting for the leading actress to appear, it gradually dawned on me that so many of the streets and houses were themselves in a condition of expectancy. They too were waiting for something to happen. High above the traffic at the eastern end of Old Street, perched right on top of Shoreditch town hall, there is a huge statue of Progress. Probably, she would have spent the early part of the century covered in soot, and until recently all she would have had to look down upon was a vast sprawl of urban decay. But now it was building works and scaffolding that surrounded her, and the redevelopment of Hoxton Square. Excited as I was by much of the new building, I was still worried that it might erase rather than release the extraordinary potential of the area. I walked down Curtain Road, where Shakespeare had lived when he first came to London in the 1590s; and then sidled along Rivington Street into Charlotte Road, which was lined with old Victorian warehouses, all in the process of being transformed into new shops and bars. Then I changed tack, diving south into Great Eastern Street and Commercial Street, passing out of the charmed circle of gentrification, and down towards Whitechapel. Evidence of the rag trade began to make itself felt. Near Fashion Street, I came across a glut of clothes and lingerie shops, the windows thickly populated with 1950s-style plastic models. One of them, dressed in a pink nightie, looked exactly like I imagine Pushkin's Tatiana to have looked after staying up all night to write that extraordinary love-letter to Eugene Onegin – a little sad-eyed and bleary, perhaps, but still full of hope – the kind of hope peculiar to a young country girl dying to escape to the freedom and promise of the city. Venturing further into Whitechapel, under the shadow of the Docklands Light Railway, and just at the corner of Cable Street, where the local community had come out in strength in the 1930s to oppose the march of Oswald Mosley's fascists, I discovered a half-forgotten little travel agency run by a couple of Asian men. It was called

Utopia Travel. The shop was on Leman Street – the street of the beloved – and professed itself 'fully bonded' and yet also 'independent', promising not only 'last minute availability' but also 'real choice'. Below the main sign there was an out-of-date 0171 number and on the adjoining wall a graffito saying 'H♥L'. I was struck by the symbolism of my journey. Slipping down Commercial Street from Progress to Utopia, I came to realise that it was precisely in those areas that seemed poor, disconnected and out of fashion, that one stumbled across the most ardent and inspiring aspirations towards the modern. For they contained aspirations that mere gentrification, and the supplanting of one class by another, would not fulfil. All too often the way we look at our cities veers between a celebration of the ultra-new and a nostalgia for the old: either the Georgian elegance of Elder and Folgate Street, or the striplight glamour of the City. What falls in between is invariably treated with ignorance and scorn. But far more interesting, it seemed to me, than our love of the past, which is all too frequently a kind of air-brushed fantasy of former elegance, is the past's unrequited love of the future, that deep desire for deliverance that has not yet been met.

It was very nearly three months later, sometime in May, when I finally bumped into Charlotte again. We met one solitary night on Brick Lane. Above us, the disused bridge loomed like a great crumbling window box, trailing weeds and flowers, and beneath our feet there was the modern railway cutting, with its silent tangle of tracks. The light had a pale, even quality about it that night. Everything was uniformly grey. And because all colour had gone to sleep, the only play was that of texture: the bricks like charred biscuits, the shine of the weeds sprouting up from the pavement, the light fur of moss on the wall. The night was windless, warm. We had the street to ourselves. She crossed the road to greet me, responding to my timid hello, and the background around her was so thick with meaning that everything took on a detailed, finicky quality. It felt as if we had entered the frame of an old engraving – one of those picturesque scenes depicting the crumbling outskirts of some seventeenth-century Italian town, complete with birds and trees, a river, and a little ruined tower – and that she and I were the single couple at its centre, caught in a silver moment of repose.

She was on her way to meet some friends, she said, but was quite happy to stay and chat for a moment. So we talked a little about what we had been doing. And she was as kind – and lovely – as ever. She told me that she was going to apply for a grant to do a PhD on African museums, looking at the various ways African people thought about their cultural heritage. She wanted to examine how the West might have interfered with that relationship, and be interfering still.

It was a troubling experience to see and hear her again; it threatened to undo all those months of convalescence at a stroke. And when the time came for me to talk about my own life, every sentence I came out with, no matter how hard I tried, always seemed to have some little hook to it, some slight suggestion that she and I had an enormous amount in common with one another, and were fated to be together. I got a sudden snapshot of myself in the security camera of my mind: it was an image of the kind of man who accosted women on dark nights; a freeze-frame portrait of myself as a stalker. But there was no reflection of this image in Charlotte's eyes, for she remained as natural and easy as ever, a perfect picture of grace and self-composure. And as the conversation went on, I realised that I could not inflict this phantom plotting upon her – or myself – any longer – and so I asked her a couple of direct questions designed to set my mind at rest.

How strange it was, I thought, to be hanging upon her every word, to be experiencing this conversation as a kind of crisis, and yet to be well aware that, for her, it was but a temporary distraction on the way to the pub.

She replied to my questions willingly. Yes, she was very happy with her boyfriend. They had been together for a long time. And as to the possibility of she and I having some kind of relationship in the future, she only said 'Well, it doesn't seem likely,' before adding, 'but I am very flattered all the same.' There was a little more small-talk, and then she said, gently but firmly, 'I am sorry. I am going to have to go now, but it was very nice to see you again.'

The shivering of my crystal city had long been overdue, but Charlotte had broken the spell so gently, that I did not feel entirely bereft. Somehow or other, simply by choosing to live among the picturesque environment of Brick Lane, she had left me with a number of beautiful fragments to keep for the future. I looked around at the disused railway arch towering above me. Some people always want to rebuild ruins; others prefer to demolish them. But to me, at that moment, this arch was absolutely perfect in its imperfection. Somehow or other, it offered me a means of entertaining loss that made loss itself seem entertaining; it succeeded in giving nonfulfilment an aesthetic form. By being so patient with my continued attentions, Charlotte had taught me that to identify a particular person, and then find them unattainable, is not necessarily the most negative experience in the world; indeed that it might teach one certain things that one could never learn either by possessing them or by losing them, such as the meaning and value of distance – and of keeping distant dreams. That was what I had got from our final conversation. But what can it have possibly meant to her? Perhaps she thought it odd that such a slender acquaintance should have declared himself to her in this strange, formal fashion. Perhaps it happens to her all the time. Probably she didn't give our encounter much more than a moment's thought. Ah – but to me it was a sweet release. At last I felt quit.